Er

The A.S.K. Principle brings us to the heart of prayer, and there we find Jesus. This is how Jesus prayed as He walked the rugged byways of Galilee. Author Peter Gardner clearly lays out the pattern and principles for prayer that Jesus taught. By drawing from his own experience and a wealth of scriptures on the topic, Gardner presents a theologically sound clarion call to prayer. Will you take up the call?

David Kitz, award-winning author of
The Soldier Who Killed a King

After serving my country for 25 years, it's really nice to sit down and have a "Spiritual Vitamin" There are "many" sound points in this book. Pray, and Find God.

Jason D. Jenkins
1SGT Ret, 25 yrs, 2 time combat Vet
101st Abn Div, AASLT, Ft. Campbell, KY.

The A.S.K. Principle that Peter has written is a superb help in ones seeing greater effects in their prayer life. You will appreciate the valuable insights he has discovered in his own life as he takes one through the scriptures on a wonderful discovery of how to know God answers prayer. Enjoy the journey with my friend Peter Gardner.

Rev. Bruce Klapp
Pastor, Abundant Life Chapel Dows, Iowa
Former Dean of Kingsway College
International Des Moines, Iowa

I have known Pete Gardner for over twenty years. I have watched him serve in several capacities of ministry over the years. This book is coming from a writer who has taken his own journey in following God's destiny for his life. Peter Gardner is like many of who have pursued God in our lives. If you can see the paths behind each of our journey you will find joys, victories, failures, hopes and disappointments. I know that you will be blessed as you flip the pages of this book. I pray that it will help you on your journey.

Evangelist Robert Newton
Founder & President of Powerhouse Ministries

I endorse the book you have written for it is *"A testimony of a life well lived which gives validity to the practice and power of prayer."*

Dr. Ronald L. Breese, Assistant Executive Overseer,
Kingsway Fellowship International

the
A.S.K.
PRINCIPLE

the
A.S.K.
PRINCIPLE

Developing an Effective Prayer Life

Psalmist Ministries

Singing and Preaching for the King of Kings

Pete Gardner

Psalmist and Evangelist

707 3rd Ave NE
Belmond, Iowa 50421

PH: 641-430-1688
pgard7@gmail.com

PETER T. GARDNER

XULON PRESS ELITE

Xulon Press Elite
2301 Lucien Way #415
Maitland, FL 32751
407.339.4217
www.xulonpress.com

Unless otherwise indicated, Scripture quotations taken from the King James Version (KJV)–*public domain.*

Printed in the United States of America.

ISBN-13: 978-1-54565-143-8

Table of Contents

Dedications

This book is dedicated to my wonderful wife Janeen, who was the ultimate caretaker during my bout with Cancer in 2016-2018. It was her love and support that helped me get through that time, which is when this book was written. She has been my biggest encourager in writing this book and is a role model for me in hearing the spirit's voice. I love you sweetheart.

It is also dedicated to my best friend of 60+ years, Jason Jenkins. His prayer support and friendship through this battle held me up and kept me going. His belief in my abilities to write spurred me on from day to day.

Both of them have invested their lives in this book through their prayers and undying love.

Foreword
By Karla Atkins

"And he withdrew himself into the wilderness, and prayed"
(Luke 5:16, KJV).

"...Father, I thank thee that thou hast heard me"
(John 11:41b).

L ife is hard.

    I can't imagine what it's like not to talk to God and not have Him hear me. For as long as I can remember, I've been conversing with the Creator of all things. My earliest recollection was as a preschooler, when I was afraid, looking out the window. I remember looking up at the stars and saying, "If you are real, help me." That simple prayer sparked a lifetime of prayers about everything from the Thanksgiving turkey not being too dry, to healing for my loved ones dying of cancer.

That's why I'm honored and excited to write the foreword for this book on prayer. I've known Peter T. Gardner (his friends call him Pete, but I call him Peter Temple – what a great middle name!) since 1989 when my husband accepted the pastorate of a small rural church in Iowa. Pete was a Sunday School teacher and song leader. I have many fond memories of having deep conversations about God and theology with Pete. He is the first to admit he's not perfect, a sinner like the rest of us, but this gifted teacher and songwriter is a friend of God. I'm thrilled to introduce this hard-working man of God to his readers and know you will be blessed to read what God has shown him regarding prayer.

Without prayer, I couldn't survive long on this earth. Battling the grip of clinical depression for much of my life, I've found myself mourning and longing for relief from sorrow and pain too often. The only way I've survived the pain of family tragedies is through prayer. I navigated the stormy seas of marriage to a pastor and the life of a pastor's wife with the anointed compass of prayer. Raising five children, one with mental illness and twins with autism, was only accomplished through the power of the blessed comfort of prayer.

Too often I've felt I am not meant for this world. Were it not for prayer, and the comfort that comes from the Holy Spirit when I pray, I would not be writing this foreword today. That's one important reason why this book is important.

People need hope. Their lives depend on it. The hope that prayer brings cannot be underestimated or undervalued. It has always been this way. Solomon, the wisest of his time, travailed in Ecclesiastes chapter four that it would be better if the oppressed were not born. Sorrow is everywhere we turn. Worry grips parents concerned for their children. Fear grips nations over nuclear war and climate change. Without the hope of prayer, how do they face it and emerge victorious?

As I write this, someone is battling thoughts of suicide. There are more than twice the number of suicides than homicides in the United States. The latest report from the Centers for Disease Control states that in North Dakota alone, the suicide rate has jumped more than 57 percent. Rural county rates are higher than ever. It is now the tenth leading cause of death, and for people aged 15-35 it is the second-leading cause of death. *People need the hope of prayer!*

I believe that God can handle our hard questions. It's not as if He doesn't already know what we're thinking. He has broader shoulders than our mind can fathom. He is never surprised by our concerns. Wrestling with God about parenting, marriage, friendships and more is what God wants us to do. Jesus Himself prayed in agony in the Garden of Gethsemane, sweat drops of blood pouring from him. It is a scientific fact that under extreme mental pressure, our pores will dilate, and we will sweat blood. The medical term for this is Hematidrosis. Think of it. The Son of God, our Savior, Jesus Christ *shed His blood while praying for **us***.

If Jesus, the Son of God Himself, found it necessary to converse with God, what makes us think we don't need to pray? I'm convinced that without prayer, none of us can remain faithful to the calling on our lives. Prayer opens the portal to Holy Spirit power, to assurance and peace that surpasses any this world can offer. Hebrews 10:19-22 says: *Having therefore, brethren, boldness to enter into the holiest by the blood of Jesus, By a new and living way, which he hath consecrated for us, through the veil, that is to say, his flesh; And having an high priest over the house of God; Let us draw near with a true heart in full assurance of faith, having our hearts sprinkled from an evil conscience, and our bodies washed with pure water"* (KJV).

Think of it. We have full access to heaven by the blood of Jesus. The high priest of the law could only go into the holy of holies once a year. We get access to the holiest place in heaven every single day! We have this available to us 24/7 – but how often do we use it? How often do we even say hello to our creator, leave alone access His Power that is so freely given?

I often wonder what could happen if every Christian on earth would pray as instructed. It would be electrifying to see. There are enough needs in this world to "pray without ceasing"

(1 Thessalonians 5:17). Just another reason to read this treatise on prayer.

In the pages of this book, may you be as encouraged as I was. God has ears to hear us, and a heart to heal us. He longs to hear your voice and whisper His secrets to you. As He tells us in Jeremiah 33:3: *Call unto me, and I will answer thee, and show thee great and mighty things, which thou knowest not.*

I can't think of anything more exhilarating than knowing God's secrets, can you? They're there for you to hear.

All you need do is ask.

Karla Akins, D. Ch. Ed.
Author, speaker, teacher, ACFW-Indiana President

"Author of *A Pair of Miracles*, and *The Pastor's Wife Wears Biker Boots*" Karla Akins,
KarlaAkins.com

Acknowledgements

There are many people who have been mentors to me through the years and thus have contributed heavily to this book. Their instruction in prayer and living the Christian life have been invaluable.

To Pastor David Heintzelman who taught me the power of thinking good of myself for 2 years after I accepted Christ as my Savior. I had lunch with him once a week as I worked to rid myself of the negative and hurtful tongue I had carried with me all my life. He was an amazing man who I will always remember for the time he took with me.

To Pastors Clarence DeBoef and Jim Olson, who allowed me to start to share the gospel with others. They brought me to my first prison ministry and encouraged me to seek out opportunities to preach. They also started using me to lead worship, which was a bold step on their part. I am forever grateful.

To Evangelist and Prophet Robert Miller who allowed me to lead worship for him every year at Fredonia Camp Meeting back in the 80's. Brother Miller and I had many deep discussions and I learned so much from him. He was a powerful man of God and is now sitting in glory and reaping His reward.

To Pastor Troy Morrison who taught me the heart of worship and to wait on the Lord in prayer. This man was the one who really filled my heart with His praises and mentored me in effective worship leadership in our church. He also was always willing to spend whatever time it took at the altar to pray someone through. His wife, Mary Grace, was just that – full of grace. Many years later Troy took time to visit me when I was at Pure Life Ministries. That was such an encouragement. I love you Troy.

To Pastor Paul Mills who taught me to use my voice for God's glory. Buying tapes and singing in services added to my ministry outreach in several ways and brought me to a place where I could better sense the presence of God.

To Pastor Eddie Akins who taught me how to play the guitar and guided me through several seminary courses with Kingsway International Theological Seminar. Eddie is still a good friend and continues to encourage my music and songwriting. His wife Karla wrote the forward for this book and helped me to put my first song together many years ago. I love these two so much!

To Pastor Mark Pluff who taught me that you must stay true to your convictions no matter what the cost. He helped me get through one of the darkest times in my Christian walk with love and grace. I am forever indebted to him for the love he showed me then and still shows me today.

To Pastor Bruce Klapp who has shown me grace and mercy in every way. He has taught me so much about the sovereignty of our God and the undying love He has for us. And to his wife Rebecca for the incredible love she has for the people of our congregation. They are truly wonderful, Spirit filled, God led followers of Jesus Christ, and I have been privileged to have them in my life.

To Jason Jenkins and my wife Janeen I once again acknowledge their belief in me and this book. Without their encouragement and prayers, this would not have been possible.

Introduction

I am convinced that everyone prays. Even an atheist has a way of expressing their needs to someone or something other than themselves. They too need help through difficult times. There is something deep within every human being that cries out for help. When trouble comes our way or when someone we know is going through struggles, we reach out. Major religions around the world each have their own view of what prayer should include. There are also many ideas on how prayer should be delivered. Some require a set schedule of prayer, while for others, it's more a form of meditation. Prayer is a vital element of the human soul.

I was raised in church. My mom was the church secretary in a small congregational church in Massachusetts when we were growing up. We had to be in church! I sang in the children's choir. Our family was involved in everything that went on at church. At 13, I was confirmed and started being a teacher's helper in Sunday School. A friend and I ran a small teen hangout in the church for a while. We were at church often.

We learned to pray at an early age. Reciting our bedtime prayers and praying over meals were the two ways we practiced. Unfortunately when I reached the rebellious age of 16, I wandered away from church and set out on a road of self-destruction. Drugs, alcohol, sex, and parties were all that seemed to matter. Church was ignored. Even then, I can remember praying at certain times. It is something that stuck with me even when I was away from God. I wasn't even sure at times who I was praying to. I just knew I had to call out to something greater than myself.

I remember one instance where my group of friends and I were working on a car. We were all far from God and full of trouble. We were trying to get the transmission apart from the bell housing and one of the bolts just would not come out. We all tried with no success. None of us really believed in God and we never darkened a church door. As a last hope, my friend Wayne made the statement, "OK, God. If this bolt comes out, I will go to church this Sunday." He gave it another try and the bolt came out like it was never stuck. I remember it like it happened yesterday. Today I ask myself why that prayer was answered and so many others, from true Christians who love the Lord, seemingly go unanswered. By the way, he did not go to church the next Sunday.

In 1976, I made a trip to Iowa. We attended a service earlier in the week. The preacher had me convinced I was going to hell, and I knew I did not want to go there! The night before I was going to head home, my friend's pastor came to his trailer. There, in my best friend's mobile home, I prayed the sinners' prayer. I asked Jesus to be my Lord and Savior. I was saved that night. Upon returning to Massachusetts, I started attending that same congregational church I grew up in. Two years later, on a return trip to Iowa, I met my future wife and moved to Iowa in 1978. We were married by year's end. Three children and five grandchildren have come along and we will soon be celebrating 40 years together.

This was a time when I really started to grow in the Lord and learn His ways. I was focused on building a family and growing in the Lord. Long hours were spent in prayer and in the Word. Reading through the Bible several years in a row brought understanding. Studying things I did not understand were all priorities of mine. Seeking God for wisdom was at the top of my list during those years. I became a worship leader in my small church. Some lay ministry and prison outreach occurred. I developed a prayer life, but I always sensed there was a lot more than I currently realized.

I had so many questions about prayer through these years of my walk with the Lord that I decided to study and learn for myself. What is prayer? When should we pray? How should we pray? Why should we pray? How can we pray effectively? In 1990, I earnestly sought the Lord with these questions and developed the basics for what I thought would eventfully be a book. After finishing the study, it sat on a shelf at home. I was busy raising a family and growing my career. The book would not get done and the study was forgotten.

I was diagnosed with Multiple Myeloma Cancer in the spring of 2016. My treatment included two stem cell transplants in the first six months. The recovery was lengthy. Maintenance chemo would continue for two years during which I slowly regained strength. In the winter of 2107-2018, the notes from this study were found in a house cleaning session. I decided to take another look at what I had written out thirty years earlier. I found dozens of scripture references, notes to myself, ideas I had forgotten about and a study just as relevant today as it ever was.

During my illness I felt directed to start a blog which would concentrate on Bible study. After going through Philippians, Galatians, Psalms and James, the Lord put it on my heart to take this study and put it out on my blog. Ideas and concepts were added that I had learned since the original study. I was pleased it was so well received by my fellow bloggers.

The blog posts were gathered together and I realized that I now had the book from thirty years ago. It amazes me how God can bring things about. Had it not been for my illness, this book would not have happened. It is my belief that God uses our worst circumstances to do amazing things in our lives. This book is a prime example. If I had not become sick and had such a long recovery time, I would have been too busy with career and other things to put this all together. Because He gave me this time and directed me to put this book together, I believe the church will benefit greatly by the contents.

My desire is that together we can get a better understanding of the inner workings of prayer. There are a lot of very familiar concepts and verses included. There are also some things that God has allowed me to share with you that might be a little different than the way you have always understood prayer. By keeping an open mind, I believe we will all gain new insights into our prayer lives.

We desperately need prayer in this world today. Effective, heartfelt prayer that will touch the heart of God. I pray this book will help you develop that kind of prayer life and will strengthen the kingdom of God in these last days. I pray it will glorify God for the wonderful gift of prayer that He has given us. I pray this book will start a tsunami of prayer that will sweep the church, our nation, and our world. The enemy of our souls is raising his head in so many places. It's time to come against him with our most effective weapon – our prayers!

Chapter 1

What is Prayer

Introduction

Would we make it home with a blizzard heading straight for us? The forecast was for the rain to change to snow, which would be blowing in on 30-40 mph winds. This was not good. I have driven in Iowa blizzards many times. A few times I was stranded by the side of the road, having veered into a ditch that was unrecognizable through the blowing snow. From all indications, this storm approaching us had all the markings of a lousy driving situation.

Earlier in the day we started out, hoping for the best on our three hour drive. A quick prayer was made for the storm to abate. As we traveled, I kept checking the future radar, and nothing changed. Snow had actually reached to just north of our destination, and it was marching right for us!

We made a stop about an hour from home. According to the radar, the snow had reached our destination. All indications were that it would keep advancing toward us. Another prayer went up. Fifteen minutes later, I checked the radar again. I expected to see the snow right in front of us. Much to my surprise, a dry patch had worked its way into the storm center.

The advancement of the snow had ceased, and it was moving in a Northwest direction! This is unheard of in Iowa! Snow just doesn't travel to the Northwest. I had spent some time with God in prayer, and my petition was heard and answered. The rest of the drive saw absolutely no precipitation.

What is prayer? If you asked a hundred people, you would probably get fifty or sixty different answers. Some might say it is meditation to reach a higher level of consciousness. To others it consists of bowing to the East five times a day while petitioning their God. Then there are those who would say dancing and chanting are involved. There would be a few who say it's just crawling inside yourself. The interesting thing is that all of these answers are correct! Prayer is different to everyone, and we all have our own method of accomplishing it.

For this study, we will analyze prayer from a Christian per-spective. To cover all religions and all beliefs would simply take too much time. Besides that, the principles we mention here could be similar in other religious practices. Prayer is a universal right of all human beings. To many it flows freely. Others have to labor a little harder to get their prayer time in. Different methods are used all the time. Everyone can tailor these principles to their specific needs.

When you ask Google to define prayer, the definition you receive is *"a solemn request for help or an expression of thanks addressed to God or an object of worship."*

Wikipedia carries this definition:

"Prayer (from the Latin precari "to ask earnestly, beg, entreat") [1] is an invocation or act that seeks to activate a rapport with an object of worship through deliberate communication."

In the Bible, the Hebrew Old Testament word used for prayer is "**tephillah**." This word means to entreat, supplicate, or intercede for someone else. It can also be a spiritual hymn or song. It is used seventy-seven times in the Old Testament, always with a sense of reverence. Some of the scriptures that use this word include the following:

1 Kings 8:28.

> *"Yet have thou respect unto the prayer (**tephillah**) of thy servant, and to his supplication, O LORD my God, to hearken unto the cry and to the prayer (tefilla), which thy servant prayeth before thee today"*

2 Chronicles 7:14-15.

> *"If my people, which are called by my name, shall humble themselves, and pray, and seek my face, and turn from their wicked ways; then will I hear from heaven, and will forgive their sin, and will heal their land. [15] Now mine eyes shall be open, and mine ears attend unto the prayer (**tephillah**) that is made in this place"*

Psalm 4:1.

> *"Hear me when I call, O God of my righteousness: thou hast enlarged me when I was in distress; have mercy upon me, and hear my prayer (**tephillah**)".*

In the New Testament the Greek word is "**proseuché**" and can mean prayer to God or a place set aside for prayer. If you go back to the root, it actually comes from a word meaning to wish for. **Proseuché** is used thirty-seven times in the New Testament. Verses where this is used include the following:

Matthew 21:22.
> *"And all things, whatsoever ye shall ask in prayer (**pro-seuché**), believing, ye shall receive."*

Acts 6:4.
> *"But we will give ourselves continually to prayer (**pro-seuché**), and to the ministry of the word".*

Philippians 4:6
> *"Be careful for nothing; but in everything by prayer **proseuché**) and supplication with thanksgiving let your requests be made known unto God."*

All this background information is wonderful, but it really doesn't tell us what prayer actually is, does it? The definitions and the Biblical words don't tell us how to go about praying. We are not told how to accomplish prayer in a practical way. That is what we will attempt to do with this study.

This chapter will focus on what prayer is. We will look at four methods of defining prayer, each a little different than the others. Investigating the scriptures to show how these four principles do the best to define prayer will be the focus. These four areas are conversation with God, communication with God, faith-in-action, and the core principal of this book – the A.S.K. Principle. In the ensuing pages, we will look at each one of these individually. Hopefully, this will give us all a better understanding of what prayer really is.

Prayer is a Conversation with God

Are you a conversation starter? Can you keep a conversation interesting? Some people just have a knack for carrying on a good conversation. They have a natural inquisitiveness that knows the right questions to ask. When I was a salesman traveling in my car, I listened to a talk show host named Jan Michelsen on WHO in Des Moines. He was exceptional because he always had a follow-up question. You learned a lot about the guests because of his skills. I marveled at the ability he had to stay focused with any person on any subject. He also brought out the best in people. That is why his talk show was so successful.

I am not a very good conversationalist. Finding that opening question and knowing what to say next is difficult for me. Unless it's somebody I know, the right questions are not top-of-mind. When I was selling magazine ads, I attended networking meetings held by local Chambers of Commerce and other organizations. Meeting new people was the goal. Saying, "Hi," and meeting them is one thing. Getting them to talk is another, especially when you don't know them. I was usually pretty good at talking to them on a business level, but transitioning to the personal side was more difficult. All of it is part of a good conversation.

Prayer can be a conversation with God. It can be a give and take on many different levels if we are keenly in tune with the Holy Spirit. The biggest problem we have is taking the time to listen to God in the middle of our prayers. Requests seem to be what we offer up, and that is a one-way street. There are many examples of conversations with God in the Bible. Here are just a few:

Gen 3:9-13 - Adam and God have a conversation about eating from the Tree of Life.

Gen 4:9-15 - Cain and God discuss Abel and the consequences of his disappearance.

Gen 17:15-19 - Sarah discusses with God about having a child in her old age.

Gen 18:23-33 - Abraham pleads with God over Sodom and Gomorrah.

Exodus 3:11-4:17 - Probably the longest conversation in the Bible was Moses and God when Moses was commissioned for the task ahead at the burning bush.

Exodus 32:30-35 - Moses admits Israel's sins to God and pleads for mercy.

Job 38-42 - God and Job exchange words about God's sovereignty.

Isaiah 6:8-13 - Isaiah's is commissioned to go to the people.

Acts 9:4-6 Paul is startled off his horse on the road to Damascus..

> *"Man becomes so entrenched in himself and in his everyday situations that he no longer converses with God. He just takes his request to God and then leaves without listening."*

Many of the prophets held short conversations with God. One of the things I notice is that the further we read through the Old Testament, the less we see people having conversations with God. Man becomes so entrenched in himself and in his everyday situations that he no longer converses with God. He just takes his request to God and then leaves without listening. Today, people come to God with their requests and then walk away, not taking the time to listen to what He has to say.

I think that God wants to have conversations with us. He wants to speak to us even more than we want to speak to Him. He wants to ask us questions and see where our hearts are. If you look at the Psalms closely, you will see several times that David speaks, and the Lord speaks within the same Psalm. This is the type of prayer that we should be praying, allowing God to actually fit into our conversation and into our words as we take time to listen to him in between what we say to Him.

I have had only a few such conversations. Each time I walked away with a greater sense of God. When He starts asking questions, they are not the simple things we usually converse about, like weather and sports. His questions dig deep into our lives and cause us to pause and reflect on the path we are on. As we listen more carefully, we realize He is bringing us closer to Himself and His will. Isn't this where we all want to be?

One particular time where I had a short conversation with God is still very vivid. I was at Pure Life Ministries and was walking on the prayer trail listening to a CD testimony. A missionary in India was in trouble and was sharing his story about a lady he had met. He hoped to develop a relationship with her despite the fact that he was married. Sitting outside her house, all set to go to the door, God spoke to him. The missionary started weeping when God asked if he had any idea how many people would be affected if he did this thing. Then God asked me the same question. "Do you have any idea how many people were affected by your sin?"

The weight of that question dropped me to my knees. I flung off the headphones and started weeping. I said to God, "No, Lord. Show me." He started to reveal to me the effect on my

31

family, and I asked God to open my eyes wider. As He did, I saw the employer who had fired me over my sin. Their business was severely hurt by my dismissal, but they had no choice. My church was the next thing to come before me. I had lied to my Pastor and had brought disgrace to his church, although it was not public knowledge. There were friends who trusted me, and I had betrayed their trust. I asked God how I could ever make it up to them. He kept showing me people, and the weight of that was incredible. Tears filled my eyes, right there on the prayer trail. I stayed on my knees for many minutes.

"Lord, show me the way to make it right," I cried out to God. God showed me the cross.

He said, "My Son is the way. Follow Him."

"I will, Lord, I will." This was the end of the conversation, but not the story.

The next morning, at around 2:00 A.M., I could not sleep. Walking out on the ridge, I headed down to the life-size cross that was erected there at the end of the meadow trail. This was a place I came often in prayer, but the weight I felt on me at this time was greater than ever before. My eyes gazed at the cross, and I fell at the foot of it, weeping again. For the next forty-five minutes, I slowly prayed Psalm 51 over and over. As I looked up, God gave me a vision of His Son on the cross, blood dripping down, the crown of thorns on His head, His eyes gazing into mine. I had been a Christian for 30 years and had never experienced anything like this before. The weight of my sin on His Son became very real to me. God had touched me deeply, and I was never the same after that.

When we have this kind of conversation with God, we can't help but take a hard look at ourselves and make changes. This type of close encounter is one we will never forget. My hope is that we will all strive to have that intimate time with Him. One of my favorite verses in the Bible says, "Be still and know that I am God (Psalm 46:10)." I've come to realize what that means even more intimately after my study in the Psalms. It means that when we still ourselves, our mind, and our thoughts, and wait on God, He will reveal himself to us.

They say it takes about twenty minutes of concentration to block everything else out. After that twenty minutes we are able to focus on one thing. I would guess most of us do not take that much time before we go to prayer, before we listen for God. In order to have a true conversation with God, we need to still ourselves before Him and then listen to Him. Then we can enjoy a much more intimate prayer life.

Prayer is Communication with God

How did we get along 50 years ago? Communications were so different then. There were no cell phones, no personal computers, no communications applications on big computers. The post office provided the only means to get a letter to someone else. Fax machines were not even around yet. To communicate with someone at a distance, you would have to either telephone them or send a letter. There was no email then! Letters back then took longer than they do today.

Today we have instant communication in many different forms. The major communication tool of today is the cell phone. We can email someone, text message them, or pull them up on Skype or Facebook messenger and talk to them face-to-face. Then there is Snapchat, WhatsApp, or any number of other apps that are available to communicate with one another. We also have personal computers, laptops, and tablets that can be used for all forms of communication. It is amazing that we have so many options available to us to keep in touch with other people. And yet it seems like we're farther apart from people than we ever have been.

Because of the ease of instant communication methods and the proliferation of ways we can get information to friends and families, we get together for face-to-face communication less and less. I have seen teens sit across the room and text each other rather than just sit next to each other and talk. We have replaced good communication skills with good texting skills, which are far less personal. In texting, we cannot see facial expression or understand vocal traits that give the words more meaning.

For example, if I would send a text to you that says, "What are you doing there?" how would you receive it? What word would you put the emphasis on? Would you think it is saying you should not be where you are (emphasis on you)? Or would you think I wanted to know what you are up to (emphasis on doing)? Or maybe you'd think I was condemning the place where you are (emphasis on there). How would you answer? This is why text messaging can be such a problem.

Fortunately, we cannot text God! You might recall the movie *"Bruce Almighty"* in which Jim Carey is given the ability to be God for a set amount of time. He finds that God uses email (in the movie), but there are thousands upon thousands of emails every minute – prayers that are made via the computer. Seeing this movie makes you glad God does not use email! Our line of communication with God is called prayer, and it must be done vocally or thoughtfully. In other words, we can speak it at any volume, or we can just think it and direct that thought toward Him. I believe that spoken communication with God is the best form as there is power in our spoken words. God spoke all of creation into existence. He knows the power of the spoken word.

I have been a member of Toastmasters International for over twenty years. This is an organization that specializes in teaching effective communication. They not only help you learn speaking skills, but also listening skills. I attribute much of my success in sales to Toastmasters and highly recommend the program for everyone, whether you do public speaking or not. Effective communication is important in every area of life - family, social and work are all affected. And especially with God! Communicating with God is much the same as any other communication that we have.

There are 6 parts to effective communication on any level. If we leave out even one part, we are not fully implementing our ability to communicate. Since prayer is usually considered a type of request, we can list these major parts as asking, being heard, being understood, expecting a response, listening for a response, and accepting the response. Let's take a moment to look at each one of these parts from a prayer perspective.

We must ask. Jesus said our Father knows what we have need of before we even ask (Matt 6:32). He still wants us to ask because that lets Him know whether we know what we really need or not. And we must ask for the right reasons (James 4:3).

We must be heard. You probably will say that God hears our cry at all times, and I believe you will be able to find many scriptures that say that. I also believe that. But God gives us a formula that will result in Him not only hearing our prayer, but also answering positively. It is found in 2 Chronicles 7:14, which we will be discussing extensively.

We must be understood. I know God understands all languages. But on this earth, we must speak the language of the hearer to be understood. We also must speak the right words, so they can understand. If a nuclear physicist is explaining an experiment to me, he must tailor his words, so

I can understand. God understands faith! Our words must be spoken in faith.

We must expect a response. When we anticipate a response, we are much more likely to carry out the next step effectively. There really is no reason to communicate if we are not expecting a response, especially if we are going to God!

We must listen for a response. This is where most communication breaks down. The art of listening is a great one, and we must all work harder at it. When we are talking to someone else, we often get distracted, or we are thinking of what we will say next, instead of listening to the response. I am terrible about this one! It is critical, especially with God, that we listen closely to what He has to say when we go to Him in prayer.

We must accept the response. This does not mean we agree with the response. It means we accept the fact that the other person or God, has given the response they desired to give.

> *"This is so very true with God. He does not always answer in the way we expect."*

We need to base our next words on this, not on what we hoped they would say or what we thought they would say. This is so very true with God. He does not always answer in the way we expect.

These six steps are necessary in all communication and all levels. We will be going into much more detail on these steps in Chapter 3. For now, I urge you to consider all of this when you next go to the Lord in prayer. How are you doing in following these steps to effective communication?

Prayer is Faith-In-Action

How active is your faith? When we pray, we are acting on faith that God will answer. Prayer puts our faith into action. The amount we pray and the fervency of our prayers dictates how much action we are willing to put in. God loves it when we put our hearts into praying. My prayer life is not where it should be in my mind. I am hopeful that doing this study again will re-energize my prayer life so that I am taking action when it is needed.

Let's start in James 1:2-3 which says
"My brethren, count it all joy when ye fall into divers temptations;

³ Knowing this, that the trying of your faith worketh patience."

This verse shows us that there is a purpose for every trial. That is why we should consider it joy when these things come up. One of the biggest benefits of trials is that they exercise our faith. Now, we all know in the natural world that exercise will make one stronger in whatever area we focus that exercising. If I want to be stronger in my legs, I will walk or run. That is what we do! We also know that practice makes perfect, right? If someone wants to learn a musical instrument, they will never do it if they don't practice (unless God decides to perform a miracle for them). If I want to be a doctor, I will have to spend a lot of time studying. If I want to do sales, I must find new customers, and that means knocking on a lot of doors and perfecting my skills. No matter what I want to do, it will take persistence.

I have been in sales for over 35 years. My current position is an independent agent for Aflac Insurance. When I started with Aflac, I needed to find my own customers. What this involved was going to businesses I knew or didn't know in order to get an appointment with the owner. One of the big advantages I had was that I knew people in over 500 businesses due to my previous sales experience. We learned a script that worked, and we customized it to our own style. Even with the terrific contact list I had and the rapport I had previously gained with these businesses, I still could only get an appointment with about one out of fifteen. When I started knocking on doors where I did not know anyone, that ratio was lower. It took a lot of exercising my sales skills to become successful.

Faith is no different. The more we put it to work – the more we exercise it – the better we get at it. Putting our faith into action through prayer helps us make it through those trials and tests that come our way. That is why we should be joyful in trials. They are the best means to exercise our faith! We see this truth throughout the Bible. Trials come upon a person or someone they know; they put their faith to action through prayer, and their situation improves. Let's look at some examples:

Abraham was worried about his nephew Lot. The young man had chosen the lush valley that was around Sodom and had been enticed to live in that wicked city. God revealed to Abraham that He was going to destroy Sodom. Abraham exercised his faith in conversational prayer with God. He kept asking for more and more mercy to be granted to Lot, and God honored Abraham's faith. He removed Lot from Sodom before it was destroyed. This story can be found in Genesis 18:16-33.

Another time, Abraham caused a problem himself. It seemed he feared Abimelech, the king, would kill him and take his wife. He told Abimelech that Sara was his sister. Abimelech thought that was great and married Sara. God was quite displeased with this, so he made all of Abimelech's other women barren.

Upon seeing this, Abraham prayed to God, and God lifted their barrenness (Genesis 20:17).

Moses interceded for the sins of Israel more than once. The most incredible one to me was in Exodus 32. Moses had been on the mountain with God for a long time, so the people enticed Aaron, the high priest, to make idols to worship. God was all set to destroy the whole nation and build a new nation starting with Moses. But Moses put his faith into action by praying to God, and the Bible says, "God repented of the evil he thought to do (Exodus 32:14)."

Joshua was in the middle of a battle and wanted to finish it, but it was near the end of the day. Joshua did the unthinkable. He asked God to extend the day, so he could finish the fight. And God did so! He stopped the sun and moon in place for a day, so Joshua would finish off his enemy. Now that's a great exercise in faith (Joshua 10:12-14)!

Samson had been deceived and had lost his strength. They put his eyes out and ridiculed him. In the end, Samson prayed to God that he could have his strength back one more time. God honored his prayer, and Samson pulled down the Philistine temple. He killed over 1,000 of Israel's enemies in one act. Supernatural strength came through one simple prayer (Judges 16:25-30).

Elijah prayed it would not rain, and it did not. Then he prayed it would rain, and it did (James 5:17-18).

When Daniel was cast into the lion's den, the king who cast him in actually prayed and fasted for him, and that prayer worked (Daniel 6:16-20)!

I could go on and on, but you get the point. Prayer – faith in action – gets God's attention every time. The truth is that God rewards our faith.

Hebrews 11:6 tells us:

"But without faith it is impossible to please him: for he that cometh to God must believe that he is, and that he is a rewarder of them that diligently seek him."

Did you catch that? God rewards those that diligently seek Him. How do we seek Him? We seek Him through active prayer! The Psalmist says in Psalm 19:14

"Let the words of my mouth, and the meditation of my heart, be acceptable in thy sight, O Lord, my strength, and my redeemer."

The way I use my words with God are either praise or prayer. When we pray in faith, believing that He will reward that faith, God is pleased. We can make this Psalm a reality in our lives every day. I don't know of anyone who comes to God with prayer because they don't think it will work. That would be like turning the oven on to bake something and expecting it not to work! If it's not going to work, why turn it on? If prayer is not going to work, why pray? That is why prayer is our faith taking action. It will produce results!

One more verse I'd like to take you to is James 5:16, which states:

"The effectual fervent prayer of a righteous man availeth much."

When we put our whole heart into a prayer, it takes that prayer to another level. This may be a spur of the minute prayer in which you reach deep down inside yourself and reach the throne of God. It may be a prayer that you have prayed for someone many times, desiring God to move. Either way, if it is with fervency – with action in your spirit, it avails much. To me that means it moves God.

I do not believe that it means a miraculous healing will take place immediately, although it may. God is, and always will be, in charge of the timing of answers. He will bring things about in His time. When I came down with cancer, many people prayed earnestly and fervently for an immediate healing. He could have done that. I have no doubt. But so much good has come out of this fight, and so much more will. God knew what He was doing. He always does!

Faith-in-action – that is what prayer is. Our words take our faith to God. Then He moves! What a great gift He has given us in this gift of prayer. The next, and last definition of prayer is my favorite one.

Prayer = A.S.K.

This next, and last, definition of prayer is the key behind this whole study, and it is simply three letters - A.S.K.

But it is not as simple as just those three letters. I'm not trying to say that prayer is complicated because it's not. It's one of the most basic and simple things we can do as Christians. Prayer is also one of the most necessary things we can do. I'll be spending much more time on the A.S.K. Principle in Chapter 2. Here is a brief introduction.

If I'm going on a long trip there are certain things that I will do in preparation for that trip to make sure I can get to my destination. Today we have so many tools to do that, that it has become easy. All you need to do is put the address into your cell phone and ask for directions. A sweet little voice will tell you exactly how to get there. Sometimes I think we have made the Bible too easy today as well. I like the old King James Version because I have to rely on the Holy Spirit to really understand it. Modern versions give you their concept in a way that does not have to be studied out, so we don't question it at all. That's just too easy! But I drift off topic.

In days gone by, the first thing we did was take out a map. Then we would chart our course on that map. My mom used to get what was called a TripTik from AAA when we went on vacation. It would show us day-to-day what our route was. It was a wonderful tool that we followed. However, we still needed a map. Once we arrived in the specific town we were going to, we might need directions to the specific house. We might stop at a gas station to ask someone for directions. When we received those directions, we searched as diligently as we could to find the place that had been described to us. We pulled in the driveway, went up to the door and knocked, hoping that someone was home, and we could get in. At this time our trip would be completed, and we would have officially arrived at our destination.

Our journey in prayer is very similar to this trip. The verse of scripture that is key to this whole study is Matthew 7:7-8.

> *"Ask, and it shall be given you; seek, and ye shall find; knock, and it shall be opened unto you:*
>
> *[8] For every one that asketh receiveth; and he that seeketh findeth; and to him that knocketh it shall be opened."*

Verse 7 says we should first ask. This is the step we took in the trip where we tried to figure out what route to take. We started with a map, or we asked AAA, or we asked our cell phones for directions. Without asking you can't get there. Next, it says we must seek. This is the time that we took once we got to the town. We might, or might not ask directions. Either way, seeking out the street and the house that we're looking for is a critical step, and we can't get there if we don't take this step. The last step is to knock at the door. It's our knocking that allows us to get in.

One of the things that many people miss in this verse comes by looking at the original language used - Greek. In the original Greek it doesn't say to just ask once, to seek once, or to knock once. It says to keep on asking, keep on seeking, and keep on knocking. You keep asking for those directions until you get it down to the specific area you need. You keep seeking until you find your exact destination. You keep knocking until the door opens. You don't stop at just looking at the map once and then never looking at it again. You don't ask for directions once you get to the town and then not keep seeking until you arrive at the house. You don't get to the door and just stand there without knocking. All of these things would be very foolish.

The most interesting part of this to me is those three words, ask-seek-knock. When you take the first letter of each of these words it says A.S.K. This is what I call the A.S.K. Principle. I would guess that we all know that if we don't ask, the answer is always no. My kids sure did know this principle. They engaged it over and over again, and they asked multiple times, not afraid of that no answer. Jesus said we should have the faith of a child. Maybe that's part of the equation!

Chapter 2

The A.S.K. Principle

Introduction

I'm convinced that one of the first things we learn to do is to ask. We may not be understood when we're just infants, but we sure do know how to ask for food, clean diapers, and attention. Our cries get an answer every time, day or night, from our loving parents. They try to figure out which cry means what. Slowly but surely, we develop a relationship, and when we ask, they come through.

As we grow older, sometimes we ask for things that we shouldn't have or that are not affordable, and we learn the answer, "No." That's a very tough lesson for us to take. Since it's our parents that are telling us no, we have to abide by their rules. Some strike out in rebellion and throw temper tantrums, or they do other things to get attention, hoping to change the answer to a yes. But good parents stick to the no until it is the right time.

When we are a little older and enter our teen years, we want to do things like start dating, borrowing the car, going to the movies, and other things that our parents may or may not approve of. They might think we need to be a little older before we start doing those things, so they ask us to wait and will answer yes when the time is right. Although we don't like the wait, we have to abide by their rules since we live in their house, and so we go along.

Our heavenly father is not a whole lot different. Sometimes His answer is "Yes," sometimes it's "No," and sometimes it's "Wait." Sometimes the answer is not exactly what we want, but He does answer. Sometimes He will bring situations into our lives to teach us the right things to ask and to show us the way He wants us to go. All of it is done in love because He loves us more than we can imagine.

Asking is fundamental to our being, and we are going to be spending a lot of time on the next three topics: Ask - Seek – Knock. I call it the A.S.K. Principle because I think it is one of the most basic principles in the Bible. Yet so many of us don't understand it. I know I didn't when I first did this study almost 30 years ago. When I looked up all the verses that talked about prayer and how to go about it, I was astounded at what God has to say about our prayer lives. He doesn't leave us hanging on it. He spells it out plainly. Since the original study, I have learned a lot more about effective prayer and even more about God's answer. There is a real freedom we can gain by studying this and knowing what God expects and what He will do.

Before we do that, we need to look at the fact that our Heavenly Father wants us to ask. He desires for us to call out to Him, and His purpose is to answer us when we call. This truth is all through the Bible. Knowing

> *"Our Heavenly Father wants us to ask."*

that He wants to hear our call frees us to call on Him in any situation, even the smallest of details in our lives. I have a job updating maps for a company, and I often call with the little questions that don't seem too significant. But my trainer simply tells me to call anytime. This is what God says as well. Read what He has to say about calling on Him:

Psalm 91:15
"He shall call upon me, and I will answer him: I will be with him in trouble; I will deliver him, and honour him."

God doesn't say things He does not mean. If He says He will answer us when we call on Him, He will. If He says He will deliver me, He will. If He says He will honor me in my request, He will! God is not a man that He would lie (Num 23:19). We should come to Him expecting a response, not demanding one. A person does not have to demand something that is promised to him and that he is anticipating. Instead, we should wait expectantly and keep our ears keen so that when He does answer, we know it.

Isaiah 58:9
"Then shalt thou call, and the Lord *shall answer; thou shalt cry, and he shall say, Here I am."*

God will be right beside us when we cry out to Him. He will even incline His ear to us (Psalm 116:2). That is an awesome Scripture to me. I can just picture God, the Almighty Creator and ruler of all things, leaning over to hear my prayer, to hear my cry! Isn't it sad that so often we can't take the time to do the same thing for those in need around us? If God is willing to take the time to lean over and hear my cry, I should be willing, and even eager, to do the same for those around me. Many times during His ministry, people cried out to Jesus, and He took the time to touch their lives.

I think of blind Bartimaeus. He sat in his usual place that day to cry out for alms. He was there all the time. But this day was different. A crowd was forming around him as he sat there. Then he started to hear people say that Jesus would be passing by. He had heard stories about Jesus healing all sorts of infirmities – even healing a blind man outside the temple in Jerusalem. He was not going to miss this chance.

He started crying out "Jesus, thou son of David, have mercy on me." The crowd around him was getting louder, so he got louder as well. He was sitting on the ground, behind the crowd, hoping Jesus would hear him through all the noise. Louder and louder he cried out, "Jesus, thou Son of David, have mercy on me." He could sense Jesus getting near. People around him told him to be quiet, but he kept crying out, "Jesus, thou son of David, have mercy on me."

Jesus stopped in His tracks. He had heard Bartimaeus's call. He asked the people to bring him forward. Bartimaeus heard the crowd quiet down and did not know what was going on until someone said, "Jesus wants you."

Bartimaeus went to Jesus, and Jesus asked an awesome question. "What wilt thou that I should do unto thee?" I am convinced Bartimaeus could have asked for anything he wanted right then, and he would have received it. Jesus could see that he was blind, I am sure. Why did Jesus ask that question and not just heal him? Because He wants us to ask. He desires to hear us verbalize what we need (Phil 4:6). Asking is essential to receiving. Bartimaeus asked for his sight, and it was given to him. What a story! (Mark 10:46-52).

Isaiah 65:24
> *"And it shall come to pass, that before they call, I will answer; and while they are yet speaking, I will hear."*

This one should really let us know He is ready for our prayers! After all, Jesus did tell us that our Heavenly Father knows what we have need of before we ask (Matt 6:8). While we are speaking, He will hear. This shows that He wants us to speak out our requests. He is just waiting for them.

Jeremiah 33:3
"Call unto me, and I will answer thee, and show thee great and mighty things, which thou knowest not."

His desire is to show you great and mighty things. When I was praying for the snow storm to ease up as we drove back home, I certainly did not expect God to push the storm backward and bring us through on dry ground! That to me was a great and mighty thing! God will do this over and over again if I just call unto Him and ask Him.

There are many more scriptures I could list here, but I think you get the picture. God wants us, desires for us, to have that communication, that conversation with Him. He wants to hear our requests. He longs to hear us calling out to Him.

Ask

The A.S.K. Principal is the centerpiece of this book. It is a simple look at a familiar portion of scripture with a twist. The first scripture is an obvious one. It is our main text. Our first scripture, Matthew 7:7-11, is an obvious one. It is our main text.

Ask, and it shall be given you; seek, and ye shall find; knock, and it shall be opened unto you:

⁸ For every one that asketh receiveth; and he that seeketh findeth; and to him that knocketh it shall be opened.

⁹ Or what man is there of you, whom if his son ask bread, will he give him a stone?¹⁰ Or if he ask a fish, will he give him a serpent?

¹¹ If ye then, being evil, know how to give good gifts unto your children, how much more shall your Father which is in heaven give good things to them that ask him?

Jesus says ask, and you shall receive. It doesn't get much clearer than that. Remember this word Ask in the Greek is a word that means keep on asking until you receive. That would be a literal translation of this verse. Some of the preaching that's out there today says if you don't receive what you want after the first asking, you don't have enough faith. Personally, I believe that it takes more faith to ask again and again and again because it shows that we trust God to come through for us. Often, He wants to teach us patience through our request. He tries our faith (James 1:2-4) to bring patience out in our lives.

Then Jesus gives a few examples of people who ask for something good and He asks us whether we would give them something bad in return. He says if we, being evil, (I think it's interesting that He calls us evil) give good gifts to our children, how much more should God give good things when we ask. He is just waiting for our requests, and we can know whatever He gives us is good, even if it doesn't seem so at the time.

The second scripture is from John 15:7.
"If ye abide in me, and my words abide in you, ye shall ask what ye will, and it shall be done unto you."

This is in the middle of the discourse about the vine and the branches. In John 15 Jesus tells the disciples that he is the vine and they are the branches. The branches must bear fruit, and must be a part, or abide in, the vine in order to fulfill their purpose. The key word here is abide. The word abide means to stay with or wait with. If we abide in Him, then we will ask, and it shall be done. He equates abiding to a branch that is connected to the vine and receiving its vital life-giving resources from that vine. If our lives are connected to Jesus in such a way, then this verse applies. We will not be asking for frivolous things just for the sake of asking because we think He's some kind of a grand gift giver. We will be asking for the vital, life giving resources that can make us better disciples and bring Him glory.

Now I take you to John 14:12 -14.

Verily, verily, I say unto you, He that believeth on me, the works that I do shall he do also; and greater works than these shall he do; because I go unto my Father.

[13] And whatsoever ye shall ask in my name, that will I do, that the Father may be glorified in the Son.

[14] If ye shall ask any thing in my name, I will do it.

In this portion of scripture Jesus not only says that if we ask in His name, He will do what we ask, but He also adds that if we believe in Him, we will do greater things than He has done. This is quite a phenomenal statement considering He healed all the sick, raised the dead, opened blind eyes, freed the captives, and many other miracles. The important part of this verse is that we ask in His name. His name is the Word. He is the Word made flesh that dwelt among us (John 1:14). When we ask in His name, we ask according to His Word.

He also says that He will do what we ask so the Father may be glorified, not so that we may be glorified. If we are asking because we will receive some kind of glory, I do not see this prayer being answered. Anytime we have a request for God, we must be willing to give Him all the glory for the result. This includes praying you will get that promotion, or for a financial blessing, or that your favorite team will win the playoff game. If God is not going to get the glory, don't expect Him to answer the prayer.

That takes us to the next portion of scripture and James 4:2-3
"Ye lust, and have not: ye kill, and desire to have, and cannot obtain: ye fight and war, yet ye have not, because ye ask not.

³ Ye ask, and receive not, because ye ask amiss, that ye may consume it upon your lusts."

James is telling us that our desires are not being obtained even though we fight and quarrel. We cannot obtain because we don't ask, and when we do ask, we ask amiss - to consume on our own lust. To me this throws the prayer of the prosperity group right out the window. I also have a problem with the Prayer of Jabez, which many people enjoyed a few years ago. I saw this prayer as one that was a prayer to consume things on their own lust. This is not the correct way to ask because the Father is not glorified when we are prideful in the things we obtain. Asking with a humble spirit is a key to answered prayer.

Now we go to James 1:5-8
If any of you lack wisdom, let him ask of God, that giveth to all men liberally, and upbraideth not; and it shall be given him.

⁶ But let him ask in faith, nothing wavering. For he that wavereth is like a wave of the sea driven with the wind and tossed.

⁷ For let not that man think that he shall receive any thing of the Lord.

⁸ A double minded man is unstable in all his ways.

James talks about asking God for wisdom and says it will be given us when we don't waver. He equates wavering to a ship being tossed in the sea. Think of the movie *The Perfect Storm*. If you have been on such a ship, you know it's not fun. The double-minded man will receive nothing from the Lord because he is unstable. We must not be double-minded when we ask. If we want the answer from God we must have all the faith in the world that God will answer. No matter how long it takes, we must pray through. God will bring us the wisdom we need in His due time.

Our next scripture comes from 1st John 3:22.
"And whatsoever we ask, we receive of him, because we keep his commandments, and do those things that are pleasing in his sight."

We ask and we receive because we keep His commandments and do those things that are pleasing in His sight. This is the scripture a lot of people like to just pass over, thinking that He will just answer our request because we asked, like He owed it to us or something. God is not some big Santa Claus in the sky. He is the King of Kings and Lord of Lords, the creator of all things. He answers when He decides to answer and how He decides to answer. We should come expecting but know that it is only through His grace that He provides things through our prayers. He tells us very plainly here that keeping His commands and doing things pleasing in His sight are prerequisites to answered prayer.

Now, I'm not trying to say that God does not answer the prayers of the destitute and the lonely. Psalm 102:17 says he regards the prayers of the destitute. He wants to answer their prayers. Psalm 51:17 tells us that the Lord loves a broken spirit and a contrite heart. He will hear the prayers of people in that condition whether they are saved or sinners.

Now let's go to 1 John 5:14-15:
"And this is the confidence that we have in him, that, if we ask any thing according to his will, he heareth us:

[15] And if we know that he hears us, whatsoever we ask, we know that we have the petitions that we desired of him."

Do you have this confidence that if you ask according to His will, he hears you? Are you confident of that? I am! His will is the written word of God, and our prayers need to be in line with scripture to secure an answer. If we are confident that He hears, that means we know that He hears us. Whatsoever we ask, we will have. This is because God honors His word. Psalm 138:2 says: "I will worship toward thy holy temple, and praise thy name for thy lovingkindness and for thy truth: for thou hast magnified thy word above all thy name."

Turn to Matthew 21:22.
"And all things, whatsoever ye shall ask in prayer, believing, ye shall receive."

Jesus says that all things that we ask in prayer, if we believe, we will receive. Many people take this verse and use it solely to say that they will get what they want. But we have to take the whole body of scripture together to find out what the Ask really means. We cannot carelessly pray for anything on the face of the earth and expect it to be done, regardless of how we live our lives. Prayer just doesn't work that way.

Next is Matthew 18:19.

"Again I say unto you, That if two of you shall agree on earth as touching anything that they shall ask, it shall be done for them of my Father which is in heaven."

This is another verse that is used frequently by the prosperity believing group. If two people agree on anything that they ask, it will be done. I do believe there is a lot of power in two or more getting together and praying for needs. After all, God said one can put a thousand to flight, and two can put ten thousand when He is engaged in the battle (Deuteronomy 32:30). I have seen this verse work out in my life dozens of times. But we still have to be in line with the rest of the scriptures that talk about Asking. We can't just take this verse and stand on it alone and think that no matter what we ask, God will do it.

Now to John 15:16.

"Ye have not chosen me, but I have chosen you, and ordained you, that ye should go and bring forth fruit, and that your fruit should remain: that whatsoever ye shall ask of the Father in my name, he may give it you."

Jesus talks about those who are chosen and ordained. They will ask, so He may give it to them. Notice that before He makes that statement, He says they would go and bring forth fruit that remains. Fruitfulness has two meanings in scripture. When we are filled with the Fruits of the Spirit (Galatians 5:22-23) we are fruitful. We are also considered fruitful when we lead souls to Christ. I believe the prayers of those people who have been saved by grace through faith are powerful. We should have a ministry of intercessory prayer, which is one of the most powerful ministries we can have. It is fruit-bearing prayer. When we pray for somebody else, it becomes very powerful. God honors our intercession. (We will be discussing this more as we go on). The intercessor will see his prayers answered.

John 16:23-27 is our next destination.
And in that day ye shall ask me nothing. Verily, verily, I say unto you, Whatsoever ye shall ask the Father in my name, he will give it you.

[24] Hitherto have ye asked nothing in my name: ask, and ye shall receive, that your joy may be full.

[25] These things have I spoken unto you in proverbs: but the time cometh, when I shall no more speak unto you in proverbs, but I shall shew you plainly of the Father.

[26] At that day ye shall ask in my name: and I say not unto you, that I will pray the Father for you:

[27] For the Father himself loveth you, because ye have loved me, and have believed that I came out from God.

Jesus says we should ask the Father in his name. Up to this point, the Jews prayed to the Father and not to Jesus. Jesus is changing the way people pray. Later on in this portion of scripture, He again says to ask the Father in His name. We go directly to the Father, but we petition Him in Jesus's name. So there are two ways that we are supposed to pray. We can pray to Jesus according to His Word or His will, or we can pray to the Father in Jesus name. Either one is just as effective.

The last portion of scripture is Ephesians 3:20-21.
"Now unto him that is able to do exceeding abundantly above all that we ask or think, according to the power that worketh in us,

21 Unto him be glory in the church by Christ Jesus throughout all ages, world without end. Amen."

This is a powerful portion of Scripture. It tells us that God is able to do exceedingly abundantly above all that we Ask or think. We do not know exactly how God will answer our prayer. But whatever He does and however He answers, we can know that it's exceedingly abundantly above what we ask. It is much better for us in

> *"God is Sovereign, and He will answer our prayers when and how He wants to."*

the long run, no matter what the answer is. He has put his Holy Spirit within us to guide us into His plan when we submit by being patient and waiting for the answer to come. God is Sovereign, and He will answer our prayers when and how He wants to. Then He has put the power within us to utilize that answer to bring Him glory. All we have control over is the Ask and our attitude toward the response He gives us. Let us always give Him glory when He answers prayer, no matter how He answers. Proverbs 3:6 says "In all they ways acknowledge Him"

There are dozens, if not hundreds, more verses we could go to. Asking brings results every time. Never hold back from Asking God for those things you have need of, or that a friend has need of. He loves to hear your voice!

57

Asked and Answered

Throughout the Bible, we see prayers given to God and people receiving answers. We have already shared several examples in previous chapters. In this chapter, we are going to look at more answered prayers just to show you that God will hear your prayers when you ask properly. The reason these prayers were answered will also be highlighted..

1 Samuel 1:1-11 - Hannah was barren and wanted desperately to please her husband, who was a priest, with a son. She vowed to the Lord that if He would grant her request, she would give her son back to the Lord for all of his life. She prayed in such earnest that, when the High Priest came in and saw her, she was praying silently to the Lord but her lips moved. He asked her if she was all right, and she explained her plight. Eli understood and told her to go in peace. God granted her request, and she gave birth to Samuel, one of the most esteemed prophets in Israel's history.

Notice the things Hannah did right: She prayed earnestly. She vowed to glorify God with her son's life, and she prayed not for herself but for her husband's benefit. This is a prayer that God will answer.

Acts 12:5 – Peter had been put in prison for preaching the Gospel. This verse tells us the church earnestly prayed for Peter. While they were praying, an angel of the Lord came to the prison and walked Peter out of there, past the guard, past the locked gates, and out into the streets. Peter was free to once again preach the Gospel.

This prayer had several key ingredients. It was for Peter, not the individuals in the church who were praying. It was given to set the captive free. The prayer would accomplish God's will because Peter would continue preaching the Gospel, furthering the kingdom.

2 Kings 19:20 – The city of Jerusalem was under siege by Sennacharib and the Assyrian army. Hezekiah prays to the Lord so that all the nations of the world will know that God delivered them. That very night, God sent an angel into the camp of Assyria that killed 85,000 soldiers. After that, the rest of the army fled for their lives.

You can see why this prayer was so effective. God would receive all the glory for the victory, and it would save His beloved Israel from capture. This is a prayer God will answer every time.

Mark 5:23 – Jairus was a ruler in the synagogue and risked his position there by coming to Jesus, as the Pharisees and Sadducees did not want to do anything to show they supported Him. Because his daughter was dying, Jairus asked Jesus to come and lay His hands on her, so she would be healed. He believed Jesus could do this, or he would not have risked coming. Jesus did go to his house, and his daughter lived.

The multiple parts of this prayer that caused it to receive an answer were the humility that Jairus showed in coming to Jesus at all, the faith he had in Jesus, and the intercessory nature of the prayer. Add the fact that this would glorify the Father, and we see why Jesus made the trip.

Daniel 2:17-18 – King Nebuchadnezzar had a dream and desired an interpretation, but none of his counselors could give him one. He ordered that all the counselors would be killed if they could not interpret the dream. The hard part about it was that the King could not even remember the dream! Daniel asked the king to give him a little time so he could ask God for the interpretation, and he agreed. After taking some time for prayer, Daniel came back and showed the king the dream and interpreted the dream, and they all lived.

You can by now probably note on your own the things that caused an answer to be given. God received all the glory and was exalted in all the kingdom, and the prayer was intercessory in nature.

Although we could go on and on, I want to stop here and talk about another aspect of prayer, and that's persistence. The previously mentioned prayers were all immediately answered. God also honors persistence as is related in this story Jesus told in Luke 18:1-8:

> *And he spake a parable unto them to this end, that men ought always to pray, and not to faint; ² Saying, There was in a city a judge, which feared not God, neither regarded man: ³ And there was a widow in that city; and she came unto him, saying, Avenge me of mine adversary. ⁴ And he would not for a while: but afterward he said within himself, Though I fear not God, nor regard man; ⁵ Yet because this widow troubleth me, I will avenge her, lest by her continual coming she weary me.⁶ And the Lord said, Hear what the unjust judge saith. ⁷ And shall not God avenge his own elect, which cry day and night unto him, though he bear long with them? ⁸ I tell you that he will avenge them speedily. Nevertheless when the Son of man cometh, shall he find faith on the earth?*

Notice that the parable is about an ungodly judge. In fact, this judge had no care for men either. By saying this, Jesus seems to indicate he was a rather hard judge. The woman was persistent enough that he finally gave in, knowing she would not go away and would not stop asking. Basically, he just wanted to get her off his back. So he granted her request.

Jesus says how much more will God in heaven answer our persistent prayer for help from our enemies if we keep coming back to him. She is not praying for material gain, or popularity or power. She is under attack and needs help only God can give. This is an honorable prayer. She would be among the destitute we talked about in our last chapter. Once God makes up His mind, He will avenge them speedily. This woman displayed what we would call persistent faith. Then Jesus asks the interesting question. When He comes back, will He find such faith on the earth?

Either way, if you get a miracle at the moment, or you have to keep praying and praying, if it is for the right reason and you are in the right position, God will honor faith. Simply asking is the first step.

Seek

I loved to play hide-n-seek as a kid. It didn't matter how old you were, there was just something about trying to hide from someone else, or trying to find something that was hidden. As little children, we would hide in obvious places. Many times our feet or our head would stick out, making it obvious where we were. We thought we were hidden because we could not see the one seeking. In our teens years, we might have played flashlight tag at night, hiding in the darkness from the seeker. As adults, we started the game all over again with our own children. Whatever the age, the game was always fun.

There is no secret to seeking the Lord because He is not hiding. It is not like the children's game we played. He can be found very easily.

Deuteronomy 4:29.
> *"But if from thence thou shalt seek the LORD thy God, thou shalt find him, if thou seek him with all thy heart and with all thy soul."*

There are two truths about seeking in this verse. First, if we seek Him we will find Him, which is a benefit. There is a stipulation, which is the second thing. We have to seek Him with all of our heart and all of our soul. To me that means giving it everything I have. It's not a half-hearted thing to really seek after the

> *"It's not a half-hearted thing to really seek after the Lord and what He would have for you."*

Lord and what He would have for you. There is so much that He wants to give you. We can have the fruit of the Spirit, the gifts of the Spirit, the comforter, the gift of hospitality and others that are listed in Romans 12:6-21. Just His presence in our lives is something that seeking Him will bring. This is so important, and I pray that when you do seek the Lord, you will give it everything you've got.

1st Chronicles 16:11.
> *"Seek the LORD and his strength, seek his face continually."*

This verse says we should seek his strength and seek his face continually. There are other verses that talk about continually being in touch with God, like Philippians 4:4 "Rejoice in the Lord always and again I say rejoice" and 1st Thessalonians 5:17 "Pray without ceasing". How often is your mind on the Lord? It seems to me throughout the day my mind goes towards Him in worship, in praise and in prayer as He brings people before me. When someone comes into my mind, I know it's time to pray for them. This is having my mind set on Him, seeking

His guidance as I pray. I need to make time to seek Him as often as I can.

2nd Chronicles 7:14.

"If my people, which are called by my name, shall humble themselves, and pray, and seek my face, and turn from their wicked ways; then will I hear from heaven, and will forgive their sin, and will heal their land."

This is a verse of scripture we are probably all familiar with, and we will be looking at it in great detail in a few lessons because it is critical to our prayer lives. Part of this famous verse says to seek His face, which is the same as seeking Him, because if we are before His face, we are before Him. This verse says seeking His face is a prerequisite to having our prayers answered.

You might ask, "How do I seek His face? What does that involve?" The psalmist says "God inhabits the praises of Israel" (Psalm 22:3). Paul explains in Romans that the believers are spiritual Israel. When we praise Him, He is present with us and we are before His face. Praise is a form of seeking the face of the Lord.

Another way we seek His face is through meditation and reading His word. His word is a reflection of Him and meditating therein brings us right into the throne room of God. This is why it is so important to spend time in the Bible. It is a time of seeking the Lord, which will edify our prayer lives. I pray that when you are preparing to pray, you will seek the Lord first.

2nd Chronicles 19:3.

"Nevertheless there are good things found in thee, in that thou hast taken away the groves out of the land, and hast prepared thine heart to seek God."

This verse says that a good thing has been found in me. I have prepared my heart to seek the Lord. But before this verse God says I have taken away the groves. In the Bible, the groves represent places of idol worship. We must remove the idols from our heart to properly and completely seek the Lord. Are you in preparation to seek the Lord? Are you doing all you can to remove the idols from your heart?

An idol is anything that we make a higher priority in our lives than God. It can be money, power, a job, fame, family or even church. Or it can be ourselves if pride is a problem in our lives. These idols are not the wooden idols of the Bible times, but they are just as distracting and destructive as any Baal or Ashtaroth can be. When these things occupy our heart it is hard for us to whole-heartedly seek the Lord because the cares of this world will crowd Him out. Is seeking the Lord something that you do half-heartedly or with all your heart?

Hosea 10:12.

"Sow to yourselves in righteousness, reap in mercy; break up your fallow ground: for it is time to seek the LORD, till he come and rain righteousness upon you."

Here is how you prepare your heart to seek the Lord. First, you sow to yourself in righteousness. That means that you put righteous things into your mind and into your heart. Meditate on Psalm 119 and the other Psalms, think about those things listed in Philippians 4:8. Doing this will sow righteousness into your mind and into your life. Then Hosea says to reap in

Mercy. To me, that means to make sure you're understanding the mercy that He's given in your life, and you know that it's on going and that you can't live without it. You're depending on it. When we get to that position, we will see that we are reaping mercy on a continual basis. Reaping mercy also means that we are sowing mercy into other people's lives. Matthew 5:5 says "Blessed are the merciful for they shall obtain mercy." The principle of sowing and reaping works for everything, including mercy. Preparing your heart to seek the Lord means living in mercy.

The next step is breaking up our fallow ground. Jesus told the parable of the sower and the seed (Matt 13:10-23). He tells us some seed fell by the wayside. The ground was hard and the seed did not take root at all. This is fallow ground. It's brown, it's hard, and it will not take a seed. We always think of these verses as meaning a seed into somebody's life for salvation. But we can continually have seeds planted in our lives that will help us to grow in other areas. We need to make sure that we are always going in and breaking up that fallow ground in our lives so that He can continue to plant seeds, or have someone else plant seeds, into our lives.

You might ask "How do I break up the fallow ground in my heart?" One of the best ways to do that has already been mentioned. Be merciful. Show mercy to all those around you, especially to those you feel don't deserve it. Reading the Word and prayer are also ways to break up that fallow ground. If you seem to be stuck in a rut then praising God can serve to break up the fallow ground in your heart. Whatever the case may be, you will have much more success in seeking God when this hard ground has been taken care of.

Once we've done these three steps then it's time to seek the Lord. Then our seeking will bring the blessings that Hosea mentions. God will come and rain righteousness upon us!

Zephaniah 2:3.

> *"Seek ye the L*ORD*, all ye meek of the earth, which have wrought his judgment; seek righteousness, seek meekness: it may be ye shall be hid in the day of the* L*ORD*'s anger."*

We need to understand our position in Christ, which is what meekness is. Meekness is not weak, but it's a humble disposition, one that is gentle and not easily provoked, calm and cool as we would say. It's a powerful position, knowing that God's in control and knowing that we can call on His power whenever we need to. Meekness is also a humble position because we do not rely on our own strength or power, but on God instead. When we're in this position and we seek the Lord, righteousness and meekness will follow along.

Matthew 6:33.

> *"But seek ye first the kingdom of God, and his righteousness; and all these things shall be added unto you."*

In this familiar verse, Jesus says we first need to seek the kingdom of God and his righteousness. And then He will take care of all the other things that we have need of on this Earth. He is our heavenly Father, and He doesn't want to keep anything from us. Psalm 37:25 says, "I have been young, and now am old; yet have I not seen the righteous forsaken, nor his seed begging bread." He loves us. He doesn't want us to worry about the food we eat or the clothes we wear or where we shall lay our heads. We should be concentrating on His Kingdom and His righteousness because when we do, all earthly distractions fall aside. Worldly cares will not take up so much of our time. This is a good thing.

Seeking the Lord is often put on the back burner. We may have a great prayer life, and we may love to worship the Lord. Seeking the Lord is separate from both of these things. It is our way of spending time with God and just listening for His voice, asking Him to reveal Himself to us.

Seek and Be Blessed

Now that we have looked at the importance of seeking the Lord, let's look at the blessings that come from that. Some of these verses will be repetitive from the last section, but I think it's worth looking at them again. Nothing wrong with doubling up on blessings, right?

Deuteronomy 4:29.
> *"But if from thence thou shalt seek the LORD thy God, thou shalt find him, if thou seek him with all thy heart and with all thy soul."*

Jeremiah 29:13.
> *"And ye shall seek me, and find me, when ye shall search for me with all your heart."*

When we put all of our heart and mind into seeking the Lord we will find Him. I am a firm believer that if any atheist would seek the Lord, they would find Him. Anybody who is backslidden and is falling away from God, if they would seek the Lord, they would find Him. He's not in hiding. He hasn't run away. He is not trying to avoid you. He said He will never leave you or forsake you. He is just waiting for you to seek Him!

Do you remember the story of the prodigal son? In Luke Chapter 15:11-32, Jesus tells us the prodigal ran off with his inheritance, got into trouble, and decided to humble himself and come home. He was sure his father would be furious. But instead, his father was watching for him, ran to meet him, put a ring on his finger, a robe on his back, shoes on his feet, and made a feast for him. God is waiting for you just like that father waited for his son. Seek Him today. He has great things in store for you once you find Him.

1 Chronicles 28:9.

> *And thou, Solomon my son, know thou the God of thy father, and serve him with a perfect heart and with a willing mind: for the LORD searcheth all hearts, and understandeth all the imaginations of the thoughts: if thou seek him, he will be found of thee; but if thou forsake him, he will cast thee off for ever.*

God tells Solomon that if you seek Him He will be found. But if you forsake Him then God will cast you off. It's your decision. Now which would you prefer? Before He says this, God says that He searches the hearts, and He understands the imaginations and the thoughts that we have. This goes for the believer and unbeliever alike. God knows you inside and out – just read Psalm 139. I can't imagine that He would still want me to seek Him if He knows some of the thoughts and imaginations that I have, but He does. He so desires a relationship with us!

Psalm 34:10.

> *"The young lions do lack, and suffer hunger: but they that seek the LORD shall not want any good thing."*

When we seek the Lord, we shall not be in want for any good thing. He's not talking about new cars or bigger houses or money – the things this world has to offer. What He's talking about here are the gifts that only God can give – joy, peace, mercy, grace, hope - the list is long. These are the good things that God will give to those who seek Him. I should seek Him all the day long for these things because they're so needed in my life on a day-to-day basis.

2nd Chronicles 26:5.

> *"And he sought God in the days of Zechariah, who had understanding in the visions of God: and as long as he sought the LORD, God made him to prosper."*

I believe God is not a respecter of persons. That means He treats us all the same. So if Zechariah was made to prosper as long as he sought the Lord, I believe we will too. What is your definition of prosperity? The online dictionary defines it as being prosperous. I looked up a couple other definitions and found that it means to flourish, usually in a financial way.

I don't believe in the Prosperity Gospel that keeps coming back around so frequently. This prosperity gospel says that if you name something, and believe you have it, it's yours. It doesn't matter what it is. From money to cars and land, they ask God to increase them in worldly riches. I believe when Gods says He will supply all our needs, He is looking at the needs of our heart as much as our physical lives. These are much more important to God than our earthly possessions. I do believe God wants us to prosper in this world. Its trusting God for all things, and for His provision. He desires that our families, our jobs, our communities, our churches and all we put our hands on should flourish, grow, and become more fruitful. That is the prosperity God brings into our lives. It is much more precious than material possessions that are here today and gone tomorrow. This prosperity is a result of seeking the Lord.

Amos 5:4.
> *"For thus saith the LORD unto the house of Israel, Seek ye me, and ye shall live:"*

I think we all want to live, don't we? This short little scripture says if we seek Him, we will live. It will not be any life that we live, but it will be a good life that we live. It will be a life that contains those things that are priceless, like the things mentioned above - unspeakable joy, amazing grace, peace that passes all understanding, unsinkable hope, unfathomable love. All of these are part of the life that God wants to give us if we'll just seek Him.

Matthew 6:33.
> *"But seek ye first the kingdom of God, and his righteousness; and all these things shall be added unto you."*

This familiar portion of scripture says He will add all these things to us. The verses preceding this one talk about the necessities of life – shelter, clothing and food. We don't have to worry about those things, yet those are the biggest things we worry about. God will supply all we need because He loves us more than we can even possibly imagine. Why else would He send His Son to die for our sins. In Matthew 6:34, Jesus says take no thought for tomorrow. In other words, don't worry. Give God all your problems and don't fret over what tomorrow may bring. As my favorite author, Francois de Salignac de la Mothe-Fenelon, puts it, "Don't insult today by looking for a better tomorrow."[1]

Hebrews 11:6.
"But without faith it is impossible to please him: for he that cometh to God must believe that he is, and that he is a rewarder of them that diligently seek him."

If we come to God we have to believe that He is. After all, God introduced himself to Moses as "I Am". We must know that He is who He says He is. He can do what He says He will do. He is the creator of all things. He parted the Red Sea and the Jordan River. He fed over 2,000,000 people in a desert wilderness for 40 years. He saved Daniel out of the Lion's den. Do you get the picture? He can do whatever is needed.

Then the writer of Hebrews says God is a rewarder of those that diligently seek Him. Oh my, can you imagine what the rewards of God are like? I can only start to think about what kind of rewards He can give me in my life. Although I don't seek Him for the rewards, I know that He is a rewarder, and so I will take whatever He wants to give me. I can be sure whatever reward He has for me will be good, and it will help me to grow closer to Him and grow in my faith.

Knock

We have learned that first we must ask. Asking means we come into agreement with His will or His word. We keep His Commandments and become fruitful. Then we go to the Father in Jesus name, and with unwavering faith we make known our specific request.

Then we seek the Lord. We prepare ourselves by doing right to others and accepting God's mercy in our own lives with all our heart and soul as we humble ourselves, turn from our own wickedness, and diligently search for the answers from God continually.

It's important to remember once again that we don't just ask once, and we don't just seek once. We keep on asking, and we keep on seeking. There is no time limit with God. He will always answer in His own time. We have to constantly remind ourselves of that. Let's go back to our example of asking for directions. We have asked a map or our phone to give us the directions to the location where we're going. We have sought out that location by going the direction that we need to go and asking for instructions when we get closer to get to the specific place we need to be. Then we walk up to the door, and it's time to knock. Knock is the third step in the A.S.K. Principal.

When you walk up to a door to knock on it, do you just knock once? Have you ever noticed how many times you knock? I know for me, I usually knock at least two, three, or four times. I have absolutely no control over when the person on the other side of that door is going to answer the door. They may be way off in a far corner of the house attending to someone else, or they might not hear my knock. They might be right next to the door and answer it right away. You see, knocking is about waiting. Once you have asked and have sought out the Lord, then it's time to wait for His answer. Because He will answer. We just do not always know exactly when.

In our section on Ask, we looked at Luke 18:1-8, the story about the widow and the judge. Jesus gives this story as an example of how we should come to the Lord in prayer. We should never give up after the first attempt. I'm a firm believer that it takes more faith to keep asking then to just ask once. Consider it for a moment. If God answered you right away, that would be great, and you would feel like you accomplished something with your prayer. But if He does not, what kind of faith turns away and doesn't ask again? I would say it's not a very strong faith at all. A strong faith will say, "I am going to ask again because I know my Heavenly Father loves me, and this request is according to His will." Then we ask, again and again, listening and watching for the answer.

> *"I'm a firm believer that it takes more faith to keep asking then to just ask once"*

The other thing about this persistent kind of faith is that it can result in the building of faith in others as well. In my case, I went through cancer from 2016-2018. There were a lot of people who prayed the diagnosis was wrong, and that I would be healed at the outset. But God did not answer that prayer at the beginning. He answered prayer all along the way. Prayer for strength, prayer for healing at many different levels and from various symptoms and side-effects, prayers of all kinds. Prayers were answered over and over again. People watched as I slowly improved, knowing that their prayers were being answered day after day after day.

What if those first prayers had been answered and immediate healing came before any treatment? People would remember that for a few months maybe. They might think the doctors made a mistake originally. One prayer would have been answered. However, answering these thousands of prayers over two years brought faith to many, many people and strengthened them in their own faith. They watched as I gained strength slowly but surely, day by day, and gave God all the glory. That was a much more dramatic result than if I had been healed right away. Their persistent faith was answered time and time again!

Matthew 26:38-44.
> *Then saith he unto them, My soul is exceeding sor-*
> *rowful, even unto death: tarry ye here, and watch with*

me. [39] *And he went a little farther, and fell on his face, and prayed, saying, O my Father, if it be possible, let this cup pass from me: nevertheless not as I will, but as thou wilt.* [40] *And he cometh unto the disciples, and findeth them asleep, and saith unto Peter, What, could ye not watch with me one hour?*

[41] *Watch and pray, that ye enter not into temptation: the spirit indeed is willing, but the flesh is weak.* [42] *He went away again the second time, and prayed, saying, O my Father, if this cup may not pass away from me, except I drink it, thy will be done.* [43] *And he came and found them asleep again: for their eyes were heavy.* [44] *And he left them, and went away again, and prayed the third time, saying the same words.*

In Matthew 26:38-44, Jesus takes Peter, James, and John aside in the Garden of Gethsemane. He tells them to watch and pray. This watching means to be on the alert, to be ready. They were there to help him pray through this situation, and unfortunately, they didn't do very well. It really doesn't change the outcome because Jesus was going to the cross anyway. They're watching and praying was so they would be strengthened when the enemy came. It was so they would not fall into temptation. This is the type of watching and praying that we need to do. We must be watching, on alert, for the answer to come, remembering that God will respond in His own time.

James 1:2-4.

"My brethren, count it all joy when ye fall into divers temptations; [3] *Knowing this, that the trying of your faith worketh patience.* [4] *But let patience have her perfect work, that ye may be perfect and entire, wanting nothing."*

James 1:2-4 says that we should count it joy when we fall into temptation. Sounds odd, doesn't it? The reason for this is because temptation and trials will test our faith, and the testing of our faith produces patience in us. Patience is one of God's perfecting agents. When we learn to be patient with ourselves, with others, and with God, we become more perfect in God's eyes. We're not demanding things on our own time, and we're not trying to control the situation. We patiently wait for God to do whatever He decides to do. It's not up to us. It's up to God how He's going to answer our request. It's up to us to accept the answer that He gives us in the time frame that He gives that answer to us.

Romans 5:1-5.

> *Therefore being justified by faith, we have peace with God through our Lord Jesus Christ: ² By whom also we have access by faith into this grace wherein we stand, and rejoice in hope of the glory of God. ³ And not only so, but we glory in tribulations also: knowing that tribulation worketh patience; ⁴ And patience, experience; and experience, hope: ⁵ And hope maketh not ashamed; because the love of God is shed abroad in our hearts by the Holy Ghost which is given unto us.*

The same sentiment is echoed in Romans 5:1-5. Paul says that we were justified by faith, and God has given us peace. He goes on to say that we still need to glory in tribulation because that brings patience; patience brings experience, and experience brings hope. What type of experience you might ask? It goes back to what we talked about earlier in practicing something. As we grow in the Lord, we gain experience on effective prayer. This experience puts us in more of a position to be hopeful for an answer when we pray. When we pray in faith, we must remember Hebrews 11:1, which says that faith is the substance of things hoped for! Faith makes our hopes become real!

Hope also causes us to not be ashamed of our faith. I can remember times when people mocked me about having faith in certain areas. When people do that I might get disappointed and become ashamed that I claimed something from God, and He didn't come through. My experiences of answered prayer tell me different, though. Getting the experience that generates hope puts us in a position where we can claim the promises of God and know that He will fulfill them. That's one thing we should never worry about. God will keep His promises because He always does. Now you may say that He didn't answer this prayer or that prayer, but I would ask you to go back and look at those prayers. See what you were praying for and how you prayed. Then look very carefully at your life after that prayer and see if God didn't answer it in a different way than you expected. God doesn't always answer the way we think He will.

Daniel 10:11-14

And he said unto me, O Daniel, a man greatly beloved, understand the words that I speak unto thee, and stand upright: for unto thee am I now sent. And when he had spoken this word unto me, I stood trembling. [12] Then said he unto me, Fear not, Daniel: for from the first day that thou didst set thine heart to understand, and to chasten thyself before thy God, thy words were heard, and I am come for thy words. [13] But the prince of the kingdom of Persia withstood me one and twenty days: but, lo, Michael, one of the chief princes, came to help me; and I remained there with the kings of Persia.

[14] Now I am come to make thee understand what shall befall thy people in the latter days: for yet the vision is for many days.

Daniel 10:11-14 tell us about a time that Daniel prayed and he had to wait 21 days for the answer. In this story the enemy came against the deliverer of the answer, and he was fighting to get through to Daniel with the answer to his prayer. God so desired that the answer get to Daniel that He sent Michael the archangel to assist in delivering Daniels request. Daniel stayed faithful, and he kept praying through that time until he got his answer. It's interesting to note that the answer was sent right after the request was made, but it didn't come exactly as Daniel expected it. There may be times that God's answer gets delayed for some reason, which is all the more reason to keep praying.

Hebrews 6:12.

"That ye be not slothful, but followers of them who through faith and patience inherit the promises."

Hebrews 6:12 tells us not to be slothful or not to be lazy. Giving up on our prayer when we are supposed to pray and wait is the lazy man's way out. We need to follow those who through faith and patience inherited the promise. You see it's not just faith. So often we hear, "If you just have the faith, you'll get an answer to that prayer," but that's not necessarily true. Sometimes we have to have patience with God. Actually, we always have to have patience with God. He will answer us. That's a promise, and according to this verse, we will inherit the promise if we have faith and patience.

Isaiah 40:31

"But they that wait upon the Lord shall renew their strength; they shall mount up with wings as eagles; they shall run, and not be weary; and they shall walk, and not faint."

Isaiah 40:31 is probably one of the most well-known scriptures about waiting on God. You can probably quote it with me. I want to be one who rises up with wings like eagles. I want to run and not be weary. I want to walk and not faint. These are things that are desirable for me. It's not so desirable to have to wait. These promises are to those that wait on the Lord and are patient. We need to learn waiting almost as much as anything else in our Christian walk.

There is one other big benefit of learning how to wait on God. It teaches us to be patient with those around us as well. We need a tremendous amount of patience to deal with the things in this world. Through the years, God has taught me a lot of patience by teaching me to have patience with Him. I do not control the situations - He does. I do not control when the answer will come - He does. I do not control how He will answer - He does. I do not control the method by which He will answer - He does. Understanding this last step in the A.S.K. principle will change your life!

We have now covered the three basic tenants of the A.S.K. Principle. There is so much left to learn. How do I effectively communicate with God? When should I pray? How should I pray? Where should I pray? What should I pray for? All of these subjects are coming up. Applying the A.S.K. Principle is a great start. The rest of this book will enforce this principle as we look more deeply into our prayer lives.

Chapter 3

Effective Communication with God

Introduction

E ffective communication is essential in all walks of life. Without it, we would fail to properly let people know our thoughts, and we would also fail to properly understand their thoughts. Unfortunately this is the case way too often. Our thoughts are not communicated very well. Then people mis-interpret them and we find ourselves trying to explain even further. Our words are turned around and against us as we try to dig ourselves out of that hole. This happens to me with my wife, my kids, my best friend. I need to learn to be a better communicator!

There are six steps that are necessary in effective communi-cation at all levels. We are going to look at each one of these steps and see what it means in our prayer life. To have a more effective prayer life, we want to make sure that we carry out each step. For now, I urge you to consider all of this when you next go to the Lord in prayer. How are you doing in following these steps to effective communication?

We Must Ask

The main verse for this first step is an obvious one: Matthew 7:7-10. We have already gone over these verses in Chapter 2, so we won't spend much time here. The one thing I do want to point out, though, is that God will answer. We must believe that from the outset. He is a good Father, and He will give us what is best for us and for the situation we are in. When you know that truth in your heart, you will know when His answer comes, and it will be a blessing.

Now let's take a look at other verses that tell us we must ask.

Matthew 18:19

"Again I say unto you, That if two of you shall agree on earth as touching anything that they shall ask, it shall be done for them of my Father which is in heaven."

The power of agreement cannot be overstated. When we pray together and have a common interest, God is pleased. Even our enemy, the devil knows about the power of agreement. Look at the story of the tower of Babel which is found in Genesis 11:1-9. God said this about the people building the tower; "And the LORD said, Behold, the people is one, and they have all one language; and this they begin to do: and now nothing will be restrained from them, which they have imagined to do." (Genesis 11:6)

The people are one, and nothing will be restrained from them! God said that about people working against Him! I could easily get off subject when I think about this verse, but I won't. The point is that God knows the power of agreement, and He honors the power of agreement. We need to strive for agreement in the church at all times. In our prayer lives, having someone agree with us will bring amazing results!

John 14:12-14

Verily, verily, I say unto you, He that believeth on me, the works that I do shall he do also; and greater works than these shall he do; because I go unto my Father. ¹³ And whatsoever ye shall ask in my name, that will I do, that the Father may be glorified in the Son. ¹⁴ If ye shall ask any thing in my name, I will do it.

This statement has always amazed me, especially verse 12. Jesus says we will do greater works than He did. In my recollection, He raised the dead, opened blind eyes, calmed a storm, fed 5,000 people with five loaves of bread and a couple fish (and there were leftovers), turned water into wine, and so many more things that I find incredible. What could I do that would possibly be greater?

Well, for one thing I can raise a family to follow in Jesus ways. I can teach them His words and help them to navigate through life. I can love my wife as He loved the church and gave Himself for it. I can be the head of my house and lead by example. Now I must admit I did not do as good a job as I should have, but I can also pray for my kids every day. I can continue to lift them up to God and continue to tell them Jesus loves them. These might be considered greater things. These are the result of prayer and asking God to help me be a better father, mentor, and husband.

Other things I can do are to pray and ask the Holy Spirit to reach out to those who are lost around me. I can ask God, in Jesus' name, to bind up their wounds, to heal their hurts, and to draw them closer to Him. I can intercede for their needs every day and help open up the door for them to come into

His presence. These I would consider greater things. They are mine through the power of asking.

Now this asking must be in Jesus' name. This is important because He says this twice in two verses. That's a strong emphasis. What does it mean to ask in Jesus' name? It means to ask according to the Word because Jesus is the Word made flesh (John 1:1-14). It means to pray the scriptures. In many cases we can use the exact words. There are hundreds of verses we could discuss that can be used as prayer, many of which are in this book. When we pray the scriptures, we know we are praying God's will. Jesus tells us if we pray or ask in this way, He will answer.

John 16:23-24.
> *"And in that day ye shall ask me nothing. Verily, verily, I say unto you, Whatsoever ye shall ask the Father in my name, he will give it you. [24] Hitherto have ye asked nothing in my name: ask, and ye shall receive, that your joy may be full."*

Now here's a switch. For the last three and a half years of Jesus' life, the disciples and everyone who followed Jesus asked Him for everything, and He supplied. As you read through the gospels, you will see these words over and over again – "He healed them all." Jesus has answered their requests, directed to Him, all this time. Now He says they will not ask Him anymore. They will now ask in His name instead.

This is how we are used to praying, isn't it? We call on the Father and say "In Jesus' name, Amen." Jesus is our advocate, our one mediator (1 Tim 2:5). When we use our mediator, He can plead our case to the highest authority - His Father. Can you just hear Him in heaven? "Hey, Dad, I want you to heal Pete's friend. Hey, Dad, touch Jason with a financial blessing!

Hey, Dad, take that cancer away from John!" Because we asked through the Son, and the Father loves the Son, our requests will be answered. We will discuss timing later!

Ephesians 3:20
"Now unto him that is able to do exceeding abundantly above all that we ask or think, according to the power that worketh in us"

Here is another of those scriptures that just baffles my mind. I think we all know that He is able to do what we ask. We can ask some pretty extraordinary things, like the prayer that I alluded to at the beginning of the book that He would hold back the snow. Or the time I prayed for healing for my shoulder. During my first stem cell transplant in June of 2016, my shoulder decided to just quit working. I mean, I could not move my arm from my shoulder down to my elbow. At the elbow, I had partial use of it. I could go up, down, and in from the elbow, but not out. What usage I did have was at diminished strength. Believe me, this severely limits the use of the arm.

At first the doctors thought it was related to an injury I had previously incurred about five years earlier, so I was told to do physical therapy. I had no pain in the shoulder, so that was fine, but it was not producing any results. So we ran a bunch of tests, and they determined it was a thing called Parsonage-Turner Syndrome. We found out later from our family doctor that this is a catch all term that means they don't know what it is. Somehow the signals from the brain, which were working, do not get to the shoulder causing it not to move when asked to move. The doctors said it usually takes at least two years for this to come back, if it comes back at all. They were amazed that I had no pain with it as 88% of patients have severe pain with this condition. I chalked that up to the mercy of God.

We started to pray for the shoulder with absolutely no improvement for a long time. We kept praying, never giving up on God. We knew it was His timing that mattered, not mine. Then one day my wife said she saw me lift up my arm when I was sleeping. I told her she must be seeing things and sluffed it off. I tried to lift it lying down with no results. A few days later I tried again and could lift it all the way over my head! This was in early January 2017 – seven months after the incident and 1-1/2 years ahead of the doctor's prediction. I just started thanking the Lord for answering prayer and got into physical therapy. After several months of building the shoulder up, I got to about 80% usage, and am still believing God for complete healing. He is able to answer my prayers when I ask Him, no doubt.

This verse goes further than just answering what we ask for. This verse tells us that He can do exceedingly, abundantly more than we can ask or think! More than we think! Let that sink in for a minute. I am standing on this verse as I write this book. I imagine my arm working 100%! I imagine my neuropathy completely gone! I imagine I will not tire when I drive out of town. I imagine all traces of Multiple Myeloma will be gone out of my system when this chemo is done. I imagine I will be stronger than ever.

He is able to do exceedingly above that. He is able to do abundantly above that. I cannot even think of what that would entail. All I can say to that is what a mighty God I serve. What a merciful God I serve. What an awesome God we serve!

But wait, there's more! He does all these things through the power that is at work IN US! We have this authority within us. We have this power within us already. What is that power? The power of prayer! The subject of this book is the power of prayer done the way God describes it. This scripture will come alive in our lives when we learn to pray God's way, not our way. The prayer of faith is more powerful than we can think or imagine. Believe it!

> *"The prayer of faith is more powerful than we can think or imagine. Believe it!"*

1 John 5:14-15.

"And this is the confidence that we have in him, that, if we ask any thing according to his will, he heareth us:

[15] *And if we know that he hear us, whatsoever we ask, we know that we have the petitions that we desired of him."*

Do you have this confidence, this assurance? Are you confident that when you ask according to His will, He will hear you? I hope that you do. If you don't I hope this book will instill that confidence in you, because we can have it. God wants us to be confident in Him. He wants us to know beyond a shadow of a doubt that He will hear our prayer. He tells us over and over again that He does, as this book has demonstrated.

Then John takes it one step further. He says if we have the confidence that He hears us, then we should also know that we have the petitions that we ask of Him. Not that we will have them, or we might have them, but that we have them. Put that all together, and praying according to His will gives us what we ask for. It may not be today on this earth, but it is established in heaven. Once again, the timing of delivery is in God's hands.

My wife and I order a lot of things from eBay and Amazon. I'm sure many of you do as well. Once we have selected the product we want, placed the order and paid for it, that item is ours. We have it as far as anything is concerned. We can choose various shipping options, but we have possession of it now legally. We cannot control the delivery, however. It is usually very fast and accurate. When it arrives, we are thrilled, and the order usually arrives when they say it will.

This is in some ways similar. God can give our answer to us immediately, or He can wait until He sees the time is right. With God, we cannot always choose a delivery date, although I have known people who needed a financial miracle, and it came on the day they needed it and the day they told God they needed it. We can know, if what we asked for is according to His will, that what we asked for is settled in heaven and is on the delivery schedule.

My best friend lost his cherished Rottweiler, Bear, in December of 2017. He was devastated, and we all encouraged him to get a new dog soon. Keep in mind, this man is a two time combat vet who was devoted to this dog, and the dog was devoted to him. They were inseparable. He was, in a way, a therapy dog for him. So losing this dog was heart wrenching and almost took his own life. Also keep in mind that he is a mighty prayer warrior and has carried me through my cancer battle. He knows the power of prayer. We agreed that another dog would be supplied and prayed in Jesus's name that it would come to pass. At that moment, the prayer was answered, but the dog did not come.

I gave him websites to go to, and they had some of the best Rottweilers in the country. He said it seemed perfect, but he had a check in his spirit about it. So he waited. And he waited. And he waited, still praying for the dog to come. Then one day he called me and said he saw an ad in his local paper for AKC registered Rottweilers. He called the man, and it turned out to be the very man who had sold him Bear almost fourteen years earlier. As they talked, my friend discovered that the one male he had was Bear's grandson! Of course, he purchased that dog! We together marveled at God's extreme mercy, and I told him I was so proud of him for waiting and listening to God. Even in his deep grief, he heard the voice of God. The prayer of six months earlier came through because he was willing to wait and listen. That to me is faith in action!

All of these verses tell us that we must ask as a part of our communication with God. They give us great insight as to how we must ask. If we want to have effective prayers, we should ask according to the pattern God has laid out in His Word. We cannot just make up the way we go to God and ask! It has to be His way. This is the whole purpose of this book – to show us His way to effective prayer. This is the A.S.K. Principle!

We Must Be Heard

I can get easily involved in a television show or sporting event. When I do, my wife can be sitting right next to me, ask me a question, and I won't even hear her. She has to get my attention first before she is heard. If she wants to communicate effectively with me, this is a necessary step. If I am trying to talk to someone and they are not hearing me, communication will not happen.

The next step in our communication is that we must be heard. Now you're probably asking yourself, "Doesn't God always hear my prayer?" We can find dozens of verses that say if we call on God, He will hear us. I will not deny that, and I do believe He does hear every cry we send His way. He is our loving Heavenly Father, and He is always listening for us. Jeremiah 33:3 is one of those verses. So when I see a scripture that tells me if I take certain steps, He will not only hear me, but He will forgive my sins and heal my land, I take notice. By inference, this verse says He will grant our request if we do as He asks. The key verse I want to make sure you get a hold of is 2nd Chronicles 7:14.

"If my people, which are called by my name, shall humble themselves, and pray, and seek my face, and turn from their wicked ways; then will I hear from heaven, and will forgive their sin, and will heal their land."

This verse gives us a great outline on effective prayer. I would guess all of us wish we could know that God is hearing our prayers and will answer. I believe with all my heart that if we will just follow this simple outline, we would get more prayers answered – the right kind of prayers as we have already discussed. These words were spoken by God to Solomon when Solomon was dedicating the temple he had built. It was a grand ceremony and God was telling the people what to do if they should fall away from Him again. This just shows that God knows our weaknesses and our tendency to drift away. We are going to break this down and study exactly what God is saying to Solomon here.

"If my people"

This signifies Israel in the Old Testament. They were chosen by God out of all the people on the earth to be His people. He is the God of Abraham, Isaac and Jacob, and He blessed this nation and defends this nation even today. We should always love Israel because God does.

Those who are saved take on the same favor as the nation of Israel. Romans 2:28-29 says, "For he is not a Jew who is one outwardly, nor is circumcision that which is outward in the flesh; but he is a Jew who is one inwardly; and circumcision is that of the heart, in the Spirit, not in the letter; whose praise is not from men but from God."

Paul tells us that if Christ has become our Savior (circumcision of the heart), then we are considered in the same way as Jews. Romans 4:11-16 explains this further. Abraham was not only the father of circumcision, but also of faith. The seed of Abraham is not only through circumcision, but also through faith by grace. That makes us God's people, so we can apply these prayer principles to our situations today.

"*Which are called by my name*"

The followers of Jesus were first called Christians in Antioch. Christian is a derivative of the word meaning Christ, Messiah, or anointed one. Having this name says we are called by His name. His name is the most powerful name in the universe. This association with His name carries His authority. He gave us that authority before He left this earth (Mark 16:17-18). He also gave us authority at other times in His ministry (Luke 10:19 and Matthew 18:18-20). Being called by His name also means we can call on His name.

"*Shall humble themselves*"

Here is the main point and stumbling block to a majority of our prayers, in my opinion. As human beings, we don't want to humble ourselves. We want to tell God when and where and how to answer us. We expect Him to do what we want Him to do, like we are in control. So we pray as if we are in charge of the answer. This is not humility. It is pride, and pride has no place in prayer.

Have you ever taken notice that God says to humble ourselves first? Before we pray, seek or repent, we must humble ourselves. When we come to God, we should have a reverence and awe for Him that transcends anything else. We should bow low before Him, and remember that He owes us nothing and that He has given us everything. I am nothing without Him except a lowly shell of a man. I need His mercy and strength, wisdom and guidance every day.

Isaiah 57:15.

> *"For thus saith the high and lofty One that inhabiteth eternity, whose name is Holy; I dwell in the high and holy place, with him also that is of a contrite and humble spirit, to revive the spirit of the humble, and to revive the heart of the contrite ones."*

God says He dwells with those of a contrite and humble spirit. If He is dwelling with them, then certainly He hears their prayers. He wants to revive those humble and contrite ones, to give them strength. Although He inhabits eternity and dwells in a high and holy place, He still is with us. This should make us realize how small we are in reality, but how much we mean to God.

Jesus says, "Whosoever therefore shall humble himself as this little child, the same is greatest in the kingdom of heaven" in Matthew 18:4. Children have an innocence about them and they always recognize their inability to do things. They may launch out sometimes with a daring stunt, but usually they are not afraid to ask for help or ask for something they need. They are not like adults, who try to do it on our own and think we know-it-all.

In Luke 14:10 Jesus tells us,

> *"But when thou art bidden, go and sit down in the lowest room; that when he that bade thee cometh, he may say unto thee, Friend, go up higher: then shalt thou have worship in the presence of them that sit at meat with thee."*

We must recognize our position in God. He is the Most-High God, creator of all things, true Master of the Universe, all-knowing, all-powerful, and ever-present. We are merely His creatures, small and insignificant compared to the universe, but loved by Him. If this does not humble you, you don't understand it very well. We should never feel as if we are entitled to special privileges with God.

Romans 12:3 says we should not think more highly of ourselves than we should. 1 Peter 5:5 says God resists the proud but gives grace to the humble. I could go on and on about how we should be humble before Almighty God. This is the first and most basic step to being heard by God and receiving an answer.

"and pray"

This whole study is on the activity of prayer. We have already spent a lot of time on prayer and will be going further into it throughout the rest of this study, so I won't spend much time here. Just a few scriptures to keep the word active.

Mark 11:24.
> *"Therefore I say unto you, What things soever ye desire, when ye pray, believe that ye receive them, and ye shall have them."*

These words of Jesus are very powerful. Let me put this in context as we look back in the previous verses. Jesus and the disciples walked past a fig tree that looked like it was in season to produce fruit. When they went up to the tree, there was no fruit. Jesus says that the fig tree would not produce any fruit forever. The next morning, they came by the same tree. It was withered and dried up, and the disciples were amazed.

When we pray for the right reason, it will be answered. This fig tree is symbolistic of those who show on the outside the fruits of righteousness, but inside they are dead and non-productive. Jesus wants all of us to be fruitful, not just what people see but what is inside of us. This fig tree was hypocritical in a sense, and we must not have hypocrisy in our lives. He goes on to say that we can move a mountain if we believe. If we are desiring the things of God, our prayers will be answered if we believe that God will answer them. This is not a call that we can pray for anything we want. It has to line up with God's word. The whole body of scripture on prayer needs to be taken together, not individual verses.

Matthew 6:7.

"But when ye pray, use not vain repetitions, as the heathen do: for they think that they shall be heard for their much speaking."

Jesus tells us that we should not use meaningless repetitions. He wants us to pray from our heart, not our head. He wants us to use our own words, not a mantra. He says this is a key to being heard. Even those that don't believe can pray vain repetitions, which are words that are just written by somebody to repeat over and over again. They become commonplace and really don't mean anything to me personally.

Prayers need to be personal ones that tell God what is in our hearts. I know that a lot of people pray the Psalms on a regular basis. I would recommend that you not necessarily pray exactly what's in the Bible, although that is a good thing. I would suggest that you write out the Psalm that you want to pray in your own words and make that your prayer. Psalm 119 is a great place to start because it is full of request to know God's Word better.

James 5:16.

"Confess your faults one to another, and pray one for another, that ye may be healed. The effectual fervent prayer of a righteous man availeth much."

James tells us to pray for one another. Intercessory prayer is critical to God and critical to the church. It is much more powerful for us to pray for somebody else than it is to pray for ourselves. Jesus rarely prayed for himself, and when He did, it was asking God to help Him do God's will.

1 John 3:22.

"And whatsoever we ask, we receive of him, because we keep his commandments, and do those things that are pleasing in his sight."

This portion of scripture tells us that if we ask, we will receive IF we keep his commandments and do things that are pleasing in His sight. That's a very big IF! God desires to honor our prayers. How much do we want His call on our lives? The more we follow His call and follow His commandments, the more we will see our prayers answered. The prayer of faith is powerful and when we walk in that faith and trust in God's Commandments to guide our path, He will answer.

"and seek my face"

We have covered seeking in-depth already but it never hurts to look at it again briefly.

Deuteronomy 4:29.
> *"But if from thence thou shalt seek the Lord thy God, thou shalt find him, if thou seek him with all thy heart and with all thy soul."*

Psalm 119:2.
> *"Blessed are they that keep his testimonies, and that seek him with the whole heart."*

If we seek the Lord with all our heart, we will find him. As I said before, He's not hiding. He's right there waiting and hoping that we will call on Him. God does not force himself upon us or into our lives. He wants to bless us. He wants to have a relationship with us. God does not move away. It is us who move away from Him. If we seek him with all that we have, we will find Him. I believe this applies to absolutely everyone, even those who say there is no God. If they seek Him with all their heart, they will find Him.

Psalm 105:4.
> *"Seek the Lord, and his strength: seek his face evermore."*

Seeking His face means to be able to stand before Him. I don't know about you, but I love to be in His presence. However we cannot stand in His presence if we have sin in our lives. We need strength from him to carry out His Commandments so that we can stand in that place. .

Hosea 10:12.
"Sow to yourselves in righteousness, reap in mercy; break up your fallow ground: for it is time to seek the LORD, till he come and rain righteousness upon you."

It's important that we break up the hard-heartedness that we may have when we want to seek the Lord. We should prepare ourselves to seek Him because we will find that we get better results. If we come to him with pride and arrogance demanding to see Him, that will not work. We should be walking in His righteousness and mercy.

"Turn from your wicked ways."

We need to repent of the things that we have done that don't line up with the Word. If you would like to do a great daily Bible study on repentance, I suggest you go to Amazon. com and buy the book entitled *The Walk of Repentance* by Steve Gallagher. It is an amazing 24 week journey, and you will not regret it. We need to walk with a repentant heart on a daily basis because we are sinners saved by grace. There is never a day goes by that we don't need to repent before the Lord, that we don't need to turn from our wicked ways and come to Him.

> *"We need to walk with a repentant heart on a daily basis because we are sinners saved by grace"*

Isaiah 55:7.

"Let the wicked forsake his way, and the unrighteous man his thoughts: and let him return unto the Lord, and he will have mercy upon him; and to our God, for he will abundantly pardon."

God will have mercy on us if we forsake our wicked ways. That means leaving them behind - not just our actions, but our thought life as well. God knows all that we think, every word out of our mouth, every action we take. Can you honestly stand before Him and say that there is not a single ungodly thing in your life? I can't! If I turn away from these things, He will abundantly pardon me. That sounds good!

Ezekiel 18:21.

"But if the wicked will turn from all his sins that he hath committed, and keep all my statutes, and do that which is lawful and right, he shall surely live, he shall not die."

I want to live, and I want to live in close relationship with God. God promises me life if I turn away from my sins and do those things that are lawful and right. This is a promise from God to every man, not just a Christian. It is imperative that we get rid of our wicked ways.

Ezekiel 18:31.

"Cast away from you all your transgressions, whereby ye have transgressed; and make you a new heart and a new spirit: for why will ye die, O house of Israel?"

He will give us a new heart and a new spirit when we get rid of our sin. We need this because our old heart is full of transgression and bad deeds. The spirit of this world is within us, and it causes us to follow after the statutes of the world. If we turn from our transgressions and our sins, then God will give us these things so that it will be easier for us to steer clear of them in the future. In the New Testament, we read that when we are in Christ, we are a new creation. I needed that once He saved me.

Joel 2:12-13.
Therefore also now, saith the Lord, *turn ye even to me with all your heart, and with fasting, and with weeping, and with mourning:* [13] *And rend your heart, and not your garments, and turn unto the* Lord *your God: for he is gracious and merciful, slow to anger, and of great kindness, and repenteth him of the evil.*

We need to turn to God and fast, mourn and weep over our sin. Ask God to take it away. He tells us we need to rend our heart. This is an interesting phrase. Throughout the Bible, we can see places where people tear their garments because of sin. This is a sign of remorse over the sin that's been in the nation or in their lives. Once the sin has been revealed, they would rend their garments. God wants us to rend our hearts instead of our clothing. We rend our hearts because we are torn apart by the sin in our lives. This is a sign of a contrite heart to God, which He honors. Psalm 51:17 says that a broken spirit and contrite heart are sacrifices to God that he likes. When we are broken before Him, God is gracious and merciful to us.

Sometimes, even as Christians, we get caught up in sin that we just cannot escape. We know it is wrong, but we can't seem to put it behind us. We repent and turn away, only to find ourselves turning back to that sin again. Pornography and sexual sins are two areas in which this is so true. Drugs is another one. I know. I have been there. I can identify with you. If you are in a place of continuous sin and desire for God to take it from you, then I suggest you memorize all of Psalm 51 and get the words deep into your spirit. This is the prayer David prayed after his sin with Bathsheba was revealed. It is a powerful prayer of repentance.

After all this has been done: After we humble ourselves and pray and seek his face and turn from our wicked ways, then God says He will hear from heaven. This is an exciting promise! Psalm 34:15 tells us that His are ears open to the cry of the righteous. Isaiah 59:1 says His ear is not heavy that it cannot hear, but our sins have caused us to be hidden from Him, so that He will not hear. Psalm 66:18 says if I regard iniquity in my heart the Lord will not hear me. All these things show us that it is important to come to God in the right manner if we want to be heard!

1 Samuel 8:18.

> *"And ye shall cry out in that day because of your king which ye shall have chosen you; and the* Lord *will not hear you in that day."*

The Israelites had decided to choose a person from among them for their King instead of keeping God as their leader. God granted their request and gave them Saul, but He gave them a warning as well. This shows us that God will some- times answer prayer even if it will be detrimental to us. God warns them that if they do this thing and take Saul for their King instead of God, there will come a time when they will call on Him and He will not hear them.

I, for one, do not want that to happen in my life. I don't want someone on the throne of my life besides God. That includes putting myself on the throne. If God is not King of Kings and

Lord of Lords in my life, He just may not hear me when I cry out to Him. He has given us plenty of warning, and He has given us this portion of scripture as a guide to be more effectively heard in our prayer life. I, for one, truly desire my prayers to be heard by God, and I don't want to have any questions in my mind as to whether He heard me or not. I'll do all I can to keep this portion of scripture and to study it and to know what God expects. My prayer life will benefit when I do!

I would like you to take time to reflect on how you are coming to God. Are you coming in a humble position as His child? Do you work earnestly at repenting from those things that are ungodly? Do you take a hard look at your life before you start to pray and make sure that you have pride under control? This is such an essential truth to effective prayer.

I know about pride, believe me. Pride was an influence in my life for many years, uncontrolled and running things inside my head. It was evident in every aspect of my life, and the sin that came from that was horrible. The biggest problem with pride is that the person who has it usually does not recognize it. It masks itself, and we go around unaware there is pride all over us. My wife used to tell me all the time that I was full of pride. She could see it when no one else could. I would say back to her that I was not full of pride. Instead I thought I was humble and willing to help out where ever I was asked to. I loved to be in front of people, whether it was preaching, singing, teaching or just helping out. My wife saw the inner desire I had to promote myself and be praised for it.

Pride caused me to get fired from a job of twenty years, almost lose my wife and fall a long way away from God. Pride took me on an eight month sabbatical because my pastor at the time said if I didn't go, I would never set foot in his church again. I thank God for that pastor because it worked. I finally learned to listen to my wife and got this area of my life somewhat under control.

Pride will tell us we can pray and come to God any way we want to. God says things in His Word that I believe we need to adhere to. 2 Corinthians 7:14 is one of those verses, and humbling yourself before praying is one of those sayings. Let's work to get our prayer life in line with God's word, not our own foolish ways!

If you struggle with pride, I highly suggest you do everything you can to get it under control because God resists the proud and gives grace to the humble.

We Must be Understood

If I'm trying to communicate with somebody who speaks a different language, I will not be understood, and I will have trouble communicating with them. I suppose facial expressions, hand gestures, and other things can communicate in some instances. The true meaning of what we're trying to say will not come through unless we can communicate verbally. If I decide to travel to a foreign country as a missionary or just on vacation, I need to have an understanding of the language that is being spoken. If I do not, then it will be very difficult to have effective communication with the people that I am talking to.

I'm an insurance salesman. When I talk to clients about the products that I sell, I need to talk in a language that they will understand. It would be easy for me to list off the benefits quickly and use all the acronyms that insurance tends to have. But if I don't show them how those things will benefit them I will not be communicating effectively with them. They will hear me but the benefit of my programs will go right over their heads.

It's one thing to be heard, and it's another thing to be understood. We can go to God with all the prayers we want, but we have to speak in a way that He understands. I realize that God knows every language on the face of the Earth. This is not a language issue. This is an issue of going to God with a heart and words that communicate with Him as He has prescribed in His word.

Being understood is the second key pillar in carrying on effective communication in our prayer life. And there is one key ingredient that God understands more than any other - faith. If we talk to God with faith then He understands our prayer.

Hebrews 11:6.
"But without faith it is impossible to please him: for he that cometh to God must believe that he is, and that he is a rewarder of them that diligently seek him."

The author says it is impossible to please God without faith. You might ask what about the unbeliever who reaches out to God and asks in prayer. Romans 12:3 tells us that God has given to every man "the measure of faith." I believe this means everyone is given the same amount of faith to start with. We just all have that faith working in different areas of our life.

For example, I have decided in my life to place a large portion of my faith in God. I have enlarged that faith in God by diligently seeking Him and spending time in His Word. I still place some of my faith in other things, like my bank, my insurance company, my car, my house (that it won't cave in), etc.

My brother, on the other hand, places his faith in science. He trusts science to give him the answers to the things I have faith about, like the origins of the universe and this earth. He has some faith in God because I have heard him say he will pray about certain things. If he would diligently seek God, a larger portion of the faith he has been given would start to trust God. Even the unbeliever who reaches up to God and asks for healing for a loved one or for knowledge and wisdom when looking at a new job will catch God's ear. They are extending just that small amount of faith that's needed for God to hear them.

Hebrews 11:6 also tells us that our faith must believe that He is. Why would I even think about praying to Him if I don't believe He is? I can see Him in the handiwork of the heavens, in the growing of a plant from a seed and in the miracle of a baby being formed in the womb. There are so many ways to see that there is a God. To me, an atheist is denying the glorious universe around Him when he says there is no God. How could all this come about in such a calculated manner without a creator? It is easy to believe that He is.

The last thing the verse tell us is that God is a rewarder of those who diligently seek Him. If that doesn't tell you that He answers prayers, I don't know what does. Those rewards are the answers to our prayers. When we call out to God in faith, we are automatically implying that He is, and we are automatically implying that He will reward us in our prayer. What's the use for calling out to Him if we don't think that's true? As we seek after God, most often we learn about Him through His Word. When we give all we have to seek Him in all things, then His rewards will follow.

Romans 10:17.
"So then faith cometh by hearing, and hearing by the word of God."

Diligently seeking Him means that we give all we have to search for God, His will, His Word, and His mission for our lives. We do this through reading the Word and through meditating on that Word. As we do, that measure of faith He has given us appoints more and more to faith in God. As we believe in God and believe that He is a rewarder of those that seek Him out, that seeking also produces more faith in us. We will then be understood even better as we grow in our Christian faith.

On the other side of the spectrum are those that don't have full trust in their prayers. In James, they are called double-minded.

James 1:6-8.
"But let him ask in faith, nothing wavering. For he that wavereth is like a wave of the sea driven with the wind and tossed.

⁷ For let not that man think that he shall receive any thing of the Lord.

⁸ A double minded man is unstable in all his ways."

The double-minded man is someone who doesn't ask in faith. He just asks because it's a popular thing to do. He doesn't really think that God will accomplish what he is asking for. James compares this to a ship that is tossed to and fro in the wind. I think of the movie *The Perfect Storm* when they are being tossed about, or the disciples on the Sea of Galilee when Jesus was sleeping during the storm. They woke Him and He calmed the storm and said, "Oh ye of little faith". (Matt 8:23-27). Did Jesus really expect them to calm the storm, or did He say this because He had told them they were going to the other side, yet they doubted that they would make it? The disciples at this time, in the middle of the storm, were double-minded. They just did not know what to do in such a storm. James says a double-minded man should not expect to receive anything from God!

Here are just a few verses that tell us why we should have faith when we pray:

Jeremiah 32:17.
"Ah Lord GOD! behold, thou hast made the heaven and the earth by thy great power and stretched out arm, and there is nothing too hard for thee:"

Philippians 4:13.
"I can do all things through Christ which strengtheneth me."

Mark 11:23-24.
For verily I say unto you, That whosoever shall say unto this mountain, Be thou removed, and be thou cast into the sea; and shall not doubt in his heart, but shall believe that those things which he saith shall come to pass; he shall have whatsoever he saith.

[24] Therefore I say unto you, What things soever ye desire, when ye pray, believe that ye receive them, and ye shall have them.

Matthew 17:20.
"And Jesus said unto them, Because of your unbelief: for verily I say unto you, If ye have faith as a grain of mustard seed, ye shall say unto this mountain, Remove hence to yonder place; and it shall remove; and nothing shall be impossible unto you."

All of these verses, and many more, tell us that faith makes things possible that we might deem impossible. I could go through a whole litany of impossible situations that were turned around because people believed God, but I'm not going to do that. Instead I can just use the short version of my own testimony.

In March of 2016, I was diagnosed with Multiple Myeloma stage 2. Stage 2 typically is not very favorable. But from the very outset, I believed God, and I believed He had a plan. I stood on my life-verse.

Proverbs 3:5-6.

"Trust in the Lord with all thine heart; and lean not unto thine own understanding. In all thy ways acknowledge him, and he shall direct thy paths."

My wife and I were calm, and just trusted Him. I never doubted His mercy. I went through two stem cell transplants in the period of five months. My right shoulder gave out on me for no apparent reason, and I'm right handed. I became extremely weak after the second transplant, barely able to walk around with a walker in my home. But I've never stopped trusting God and knowing that He had a purpose and a reason. In fact, even at my lowest point, I would say, "God has been very merciful to me." I always approached everything with the faith that He was going to completely heal me.

The only common side effect I suffer from is neuropathy in my feet and hands. I never had any mouth sores, upset stomach, diarrhea or any other side effects like that. They told me my shoulder would probably not start working again, or if it did, it would take at least two years. It started working in eight months, and gets stronger every day. The neuropathy seems to be getting better, and I'm still believing God for full healing in both of these areas.

Many prayed that the diagnosis was wrong, and that I would be instantly healed. I was not. Many around the world are praying now that God will continue to move and He is. He had a plan for the two years that have gone by so far! God has given me an online ministry I never even dreamed of!

The Holy Spirit has spoken to me songs and poetry almost daily. Since the beginning of this cancer, I have written over 1,000 poems and songs of praise and comfort and shared them on my Facebook "The Psalmist" page, which has over 3,200 followers. On my WordPress Bible study blog, I have done studies through the books of Philippians, Ephesians, Psalms, and James. I came across the notes for this book from thirty years ago, and now the book is a reality. I have been in the word more than ever in my life. Through all of this, I have had thousands of encouraging comments and messages on how people have been touched by these words. A few people have been saved by the words, and some were healed. God gets all the glory!

This is a ministry that most likely would not have happened if I had not been sick for so long. God had a purpose for this in my life, and the result is only just beginning. As a rewarder of my faith, I know He has more in store. I'm looking forward to the day that I can go out and minister the gift of healing in other churches around the Midwest. God has given me a platform to shout His praises, and I intend to do that very thing. All because, when this all began, I prayed the prayer of faith and asked God to use this situation for His glory. I am just clay in His hands.

What are you going through that is hard? Glorify God because of it! Ask Him to use you in the middle of the storm. Ask Him to make you a blessing to others as you weather the storm that has you reeling in life. Don't allow the situations you face to block out the mercy of God. Instead, have joy in the midst of your storm, knowing God will use this storm to perfect you (James 1:2-4)

"Ask Him to make you a blessing to others as you weather the storm that has you reeling in life."

God understands faith. To effectively communicate with God we must be heard and then we must be understood by praying the prayer of faith.

We Must Expect a Response

We must expect a response. We talked about the double minded man in the previous lesson. He is the one who wavers when he prays, not really believing God can do what he is asking or that He will do it. This kind of prayer is prayed more than we like to realize. If we want an effective prayer life, we must build our faith to the point that we do not doubt God will answer. We must know with all our heart that we can expect a response.

When we know we have been heard and understood by God because we are speaking in faith, we should expect a response. Expect means to look forward to or to look on as likely to happen or to anticipate. I would guess that all of us, when we come to the Lord in prayer, come with this attribute in high gear. We want an answer, and we know that God is able to supply those answers no matter how difficult the situation. We are going to look at three different words that are used in the Bible to signify waiting and expecting. There are more, but for sake of brevity, I would rather use only three. All of these words show an understanding that the waiting, the expectation, will be answered.

The first word is from the Old Testament and is the Hebrew word **qavah**. It is translated wait or look for or looking for. It denotes an anticipated response in due time.

Psalm 40:1.
> *"I waited patiently for the LORD; and he inclined unto me, and heard my cry."*

Is this the way we wait for God – patiently? Or do we get anxious wondering when, oh when, will He give me an answer. Patience is essential in our waiting. We have absolutely no control over when God will answer, and whatever we are going through is in His hands. He will decide when to lift the burden. In James 1:2-5, we are told that a trial comes to test our faith and teach us patience. Do you learn this lesson when going through difficult situations, or do you fret and stew because the answer has not yet come? Look at the promise of this Psalm. If I wait, He will incline to me and hear me. I picture a loving God leaning over, so I can whisper in His ear. What a powerful portion of scripture!

Lamentations 3:25.
> *"The LORD is good unto them that wait for him, to the soul that seeketh him."*

God will never disappoint you if you are waiting for His answer, not your own. If you are looking for what you want, then perhaps you will be disappointed, but that is not God's fault. He always sends the best answer, the good answer. We just need to put ourselves in a place of waiting and anticipating His response.

Isaiah 40:31.

> *"But they that wait upon the* LORD *shall renew their strength; they shall mount up with wings as eagles; they shall run, and not be weary; and they shall walk, and not faint."*

I'll guess most of you figured I would be using this verse. It is probably the most well-known verse on waiting. The promises contained here are staggering to me. God tells us, through Isaiah, that if we will be patient and wait for His timing in our lives that He will strengthen us. That means to me that He will give me the strength in the middle of my struggles to wait for His perfect response. That strength will carry me through the trouble until He decides to bring the solution. That strength will help me to run and not grow weary, and walk and not faint. I do not have to worry about falling short or about not finishing well. His strength will carry me through. In the meantime, I can soar above my troubles like an eagle soaring above the ground. I can be confident to rise above the struggles! What a mighty God we serve.

The next word is the Greek word **ekdechomai**. It means to look for or expect.

John 5:2-4

> *Now there is at Jerusalem by the sheep market a pool, which is called in the Hebrew tongue Bethesda, having five porches.*
>
> *³ In these lay a great multitude of impotent folk, of blind, halt, withered, waiting for the moving of the water.*
>
> *⁴ For an angel went down at a certain season into the pool, and troubled the water: whosoever then first after*

the troubling of the water stepped in was made whole of whatsoever disease he had.

Do you get the picture here? A group of people wait by this pool for the troubling of the water. An angel always comes at a certain season. They could be there for days, just waiting for that water to start churning. Talk about expecting a response! They had to be ready at all times to receive because the first one that got in would be made whole of whatever disease they had, no one else. Wow! I wish I always had that much faith that God would send an answer.

These verses tell about people who are waiting for something that is a certainty. They know that the pool will be troubled. They also know that the first person in would be healed, so they waited. They just have to wait for the angel to come. We should so wait for our answer from God, knowing that it is a certainty, and we should be ready to receive it when-ever it comes.

James 1:7.
> *"Be patient therefore, brethren, unto the coming of the Lord. Behold, the husbandman waiteth for the precious fruit of the earth, and hath long patience for it, until he receive the early and latter rain."*

I live in Iowa, and farmers amaze me. They invest thousands of dollars in seed, spend hundreds of hours repairing their machinery and preparing the soil, and don't get a result for 90-120 days. They know the seed will produce fruit, and they just need to wait until the appropriate time to gather that crop. They expect the seed to produce. I don't know any farmer who has ever planted who does not expect a return on that planting. He just waits for what he knows is coming. We should have the same expectation with our prayers. They are seeds planted, and God will provide an answer when the time is right.

1 Peter 3:20.
"Which sometime were disobedient, when once the longsuffering of God waited in the days of Noah, while the ark was a preparing, wherein few, that is, eight souls were saved by water."

This time the word describes God waiting! God waited on those preparing the ark. He knew for a certainty it would be completed someday, and He would send the flood. There is no doubt in God's mind that this was going to happen. It was just a matter of time. God will always wait until we are truly ready to receive the answer, never early, never late. We might think His timing is off, but it is not. His answer will come once He knows we are prepared to receive it.

I go back to the story I told a few pages ago about my friend and his dog. We all knew he really needed to get a new dog. He knew he needed one. God knew he needed one. That dog is an essential part of his life. He was willing to wait until God knew he was ready, and then the amazing happened. God is like that. He supplies exceedingly, abundantly above what we can ask or imagine (Eph 3:20)!

We see in all three uses of this word that these are not answers sent in our time schedule. They are answers that take a little while, and we have to wait until the appropriate time. That is how God works. He gives us an answer in the appropriate time, and we should be in an attitude of expectation to receive from Him when He's ready to give.

The next Greek word is *prosdakao.* This word means to watch for or look for.

Luke 1:21.

"And the people waited for Zacharias, and marvelled that he tarried so long in the temple."

Zacharias had gone in to do his duty and burn incense in the temple. While he was behind the veil, the angel Gabriel appeared to him and told him that his wife would give birth to a son. This son would be mighty for God and would be named John (John the Baptist). Zacharias was much longer in lighting the incense than normal, and the people were waiting for him, wondering why it was taking so long. This type of expectation is one that knows beyond a shadow of a doubt that something is coming. We need to be convinced that we will receive an answer. Even if it is delayed longer than I we would like or expect, we need to know He will answer. God always answers our prayers! The people had no idea Zacharias was having a heavenly meeting in there!

Luke 3:15.

"And as the people were in expectation, and all men mused in their hearts of John, whether he were the Christ, or not;"

People were waiting to be baptized, and they had long been expecting the Messiah to come. It was a foregone conclusion that He would come someday. There was absolutely no doubt in their minds. Now they wondered if John the Baptist was that Messiah, that answer to their expectation. This is the kind of expectation we should have when we pray!

But we must also be ready to wait for the right answer, not just any answer. John the Baptist was not the answer. In my current situation, I could be thinking God has answered my prayers because I am in remission; the cancer is gone! But

I have not received the whole answer yet. I am believing for complete healing – neuropathy and tiredness will be gone as well. I need to continue in a state of expectancy for the full answer to my prayers. Glory to God!

Acts 3:5.
"And he gave heed unto them, expecting to receive something of them."

Peter and John were entering the temple one day and saw a lame man begging for alms. They approached the man and told him to look at them. He looked at them, and it says he expected to receive something from them. He had no doubt in his mind that these men would give him something. The man expected to receive money, but Peter and John had something much more precious. They gave him back his legs!

God answers our request, and it is always His best for us that is given in response. It may not be what we expected to receive or what we asked for, but we can know of a certainty that if we wait on His timing, it will be the best thing for us. Again, with this definition we see the type of expectancy that we should all have. It is one that knows there will be a response and that it is soon to come. We should never stop being in this expecting state.

How good are you at waiting? Are you always in a position that you expect a response, and are you willing to wait for God's perfect answer for your life? Are you drawing strength from God to endure the wait? Are you soaring above the problem while you wait? God loves us, and He will answer in His time. We should expect that. Patience is all we need to enjoy the time of waiting. Let us wait on Him with expectation!

We Must Listen for a Response

If we expect to get a response from God, then it's of critical importance that we listen for that response. Listening is the next step in communicating with God. I must admit that I'm not very good at listening. Often, when I get into a conversation with somebody, I think about the next thing I want to say, and I don't always completely hear what the person that I'm talking with has to say. I also have other things that are going on around me that cause distractions. It is critical that we learn to listen to God. Listening closely will vastly improve our day-to-day life and our prayer life.

The way that we hear from God the most is through His Word. If you are not reading the Word of God on a regular basis - I recommend daily – you are not training yourself to hear His voice. Yes, we can train our ear to His voice. The truth is that God speaks to us every time we read His Word! We need to make sure our hearts are prepared to hear. We have talked about this in previous lessons.

Romans 10:17 tells us that faith comes by hearing and hearing by the Word of God. Not only will He reveal His will to us through His Word, but it will also increase our faith. How many times have you been reading a familiar portion of scripture, and you became aware of something new in that portion of scripture that you hadn't seen before? It's always been there, you just hadn't noticed it or hadn't thought about it in the way you are right now. That is God talking to you through the Holy Spirit. Start to recognize this as His voice, and you will realize that you're hearing from God a lot more than you think you are.

When we want to hear from God, what are we listening for? Are we listening for an audible voice or a stirring in our heart or just a faint small voice speaking to us? First Kings 19:11-12 tell us about Elijah:

114

And he (God) said, Go forth, and stand upon the mount before the LORD. And, behold, the LORD passed by, and a great and strong wind rent the mountains, and brake in pieces the rocks before the LORD; but the LORD was not in the wind: and after the wind an earthquake; but the LORD was not in the earthquake:

[12] And after the earthquake a fire; but the LORD was not in the fire: and after the fire a still small voice.

Elijah just came from a glorious victory over 400 prophets of Baal. Now he was afraid of Jezebel the Queen and was on the run. God told him to get to the mountains, and when he got there, God asked Elijah, "What are you doing here?" Elijah answered that he was all alone serving God in the nation, and now they were out to get him. God told him to go stand on the mountain before the Lord, and we see the events listed above. A strong wind, an earthquake and a fire passed by Elijah, but God was not in any one of them. God spoke in a still, small voice.

We often look for God in the hustle and bustle of this world or when our worship services are really going well and the praises are being lifted high in the church. Being from a Pentecostal church, I love it when we shout and sing praises to the Lord. I love the high praise, which is what I call it when the drums and the guitars and the keyboard and the singers are turned up on high volume, and the church and all the grounds are filled with the praises of the Lord. But as much as I love that, it is rare to hear God speak during those times. It is when things quiet down that God speaks. He may even use a word of prophecy or tongues with an interpretation in these quiet times.

I will never forget the prophecy that came forth upon me in August of 2010. We were in one of those tent revivals and had just finished a rousing worship service and heart thumping hour of preaching. The room was quiet, and the man of God came up to me and said, "Because you have been waiting patiently and crying out to God to use you once again, God is going to do a new thing in you. Something you haven't done before and do not expect. And that new thing will be for God's glory, and it will produce praise and glory to His name. It is not something you will do, but something He will do. It will spring out of your heart so that all will see that it is God that is doing this thing, and not you." I was in tears when this was spoken. I had been out of ministry for over three years because of sin in my life, and I was so hungry for God to move. Two months after this, God started to give me worship choruses, songs, and poems, and that has not stopped. Over 2,000 poems, songs, and worship choruses have flowed through the Holy Spirit into my heart and onto paper. They are still coming today. When God speaks to us, it will come to pass!

Psalm 29:3-9.
The voice of the LORD is upon the waters: the God of glory thundereth: the LORD is upon many waters.

4 The voice of the LORD is powerful; the voice of the LORD is full of majesty.

5 The voice of the LORD breaketh the cedars; yea, the LORD breaketh the cedars of Lebanon.

6 He maketh them also to skip like a calf; Lebanon and Sirion like a young unicorn.

7 The voice of the LORD divideth the flames of fire.

8 The voice of the LORD shaketh the wilderness; the LORD shaketh the wilderness of Kadesh.

⁹ The voice of the LORD maketh the hinds to calve, and discovereth the forests: and in his temple doth every one speak of his glory.

Psalm 29:3-9 is one of the best portions of scripture to see a description of the voice of the Lord. Look at the attributes David gives to the voice of the Lord: It thunders upon the waters. It is powerful and full of majesty. It breaks the cedars (these are the strongest of trees). It fills with joy like a young calf. It divides fire. It shakes the wilderness. It makes the animals bear their young, and it discovers the forest.

With these attributes, why does He remain so quiet with us? It is because He wants to be close to us and have that personal one-on-one with us. If He spoke to each of us in full volume, it would be heard for dozens of miles away, like thunder is, and it would be seen from hundreds of miles away, like the lightening is. It would break our houses and shake the land. His voice is so powerful that the Israelites decided they wanted God to speak to Moses, and then Moses would speak to the people because they heard the thundering of His voice and were afraid (Ex 20:18-21).

Still today many of us depend on our religious leaders to speak the words of God to us. Much of the time, we don't even test what our religious leaders say. We just take their word for it. This can easily lead to our deception if we are not grounded in the word. Many might remember the Jim Jones "People's Temple" cult where 918 people committed mass suicide because they believed the words that were spoken to them by Jones. They did not check out the words he spoke with scripture. Like the Israelites, we are afraid to have God be up close and personal, because of our faults and shortcomings. We figure that God would never want to speak with us. But that is so wrong! God desires to speak with you all the time. All you have to do is listen!

John 10:1-5.

¹ Verily, verily, I say unto you, He that entereth not by the door into the sheepfold, but climbeth up some other way, the same is a thief and a robber.

² But he that entereth in by the door is the shepherd of the sheep.

³ To him the porter openeth; and the sheep hear his voice: and he calleth his own sheep by name, and leadeth them out.

⁴ And when he putteth forth his own sheep, he goeth before them, and the sheep follow him: for they know his voice.

⁵ And a stranger will they not follow, but will flee from him: for they know not the voice of strangers.

If you have accepted Jesus Christ as your Savior, then you are His sheep, and you will know His voice. Do you know the voice of the Lord when it comes to you? Can you recognize it from the voice of the enemy? In cartoons they sometimes show good and evil sitting on someone's shoulder and speaking to them at the same time. This isn't all that far from the truth. We are constantly having to choose between the righteous path and the sinful one. This is another reason should know the scriptures and rely on the Holy Spirit to bring them to your remembrance when you need them.

Do you remember the portion of scripture in Matthew 4:1-11 when Jesus went into the wilderness to be tempted for 40 days? Satan tempted Jesus and he even used a portion of scripture to do it! He said, "He (meaning God) will give His angels charge over thee, to keep thee." These verses can be found in Psalm 91:11-12. But Jesus knew His scripture, and He knew the enemy had left out just four little words that drastically changed the meaning of these words. "In all thy ways" – that means in the everyday life you live. It does not mean He will protect us if we decide to jump off a cliff, or in front of a train. Jesus told the enemy that he shall not tempt the Lord His God. We should never do that! If the enemy came to you quoting scripture, would you know if he was accurate? Jesus used scripture from Deuteronomy all three times the devil approached Him.

I have long been an advocate of reading the Bible through in a year at least once in your young Christian life. I have done it at last six times through my 40 years of being a Christian. Not when you first get saved, but I suggest sometime after that would be better. The reason I believe that is important is two-fold. First, it gives you the whole story, and you are better able to connect the New and Old Testament. Second, Jesus told us the Holy Spirit would bring things to our remembrance (John 14:26). How can He bring it to your remembrance if it is not already in there? Now I do believe that the Holy Spirit can give you scripture from anywhere in the Bible, but it is better for you if it is already there ready to utilize when you need it. You may not consciously remember it, but if you have read it, it is in your memory banks ready to be withdrawn. You need to know scripture so that when you hear that quiet voice, you will be able to discern if it is God or the enemy. Remember, Satan can appear as an angel of light (2 Cor 11:14). We need to know our Bible because the answer to our prayer may already be in there.

In Matthew 13 Jesus gives the parable of the sower and the seed and explains what it means to the disciples.

Matthew 13;18-23;
Hear ye therefore the parable of the sower.

[19] When any one heareth the word of the kingdom, and understandeth it not, then cometh the wicked one, and catcheth away that which was sown in his heart. This is he which received seed by the way side.

[20] But he that received the seed into stony places, the same is he that heareth the word, and anon with joy receiveth it;

[21] Yet hath he not root in himself, but dureth for a while: for when tribulation or persecution ariseth because of the word, by and by he is offended.

[22] He also that received seed among the thorns is he that heareth the word; and the care of this world, and the deceitfulness of riches, choke the word, and he becometh unfruitful.

[23] But he that received seed into the good ground is he that heareth the word, and understandeth it; which also beareth fruit, and bringeth forth, some an hundredfold, some sixty, some thirty.

Jesus lets us know here how important listening is. We will also refer to this portion of scripture in our next lesson – Accepting the Response. The first person is the one who receives the seed – the Word – by the way side. The way side is hard, trampled down dirt, and the seed cannot take root at all. It is gobbled up by birds the moment it is cast down. These are those who think they already have all the answers and are not even willing to listen to exhortation or another differing view. There is a lot of pride in this person, and I have been there in the past. When God tries to speak to them, if it's not what they want to hear, they don't let it in at all. They are almost in a place where they refuse to hear the voice of the Lord, even though they have prayed and asked for a response. If it's not what they want, they won't hear it.

The second one is the one represented by the stony ground. The Word comes in and takes root, but when tough times come, it is forgotten and cast off. The voice of the Lord makes a first impression, but if it does not take care of the trial or test completely, that person forgets the mercy that has already been extended and backs off from what God has said. Boy, would I be in trouble if I did not recognize the little mercies (and big ones) He has granted me and spoken to me while going through this cancer business. His voice is always speaking, guiding and directing. I keep asking for healing, complete healing, and slowly but surely it is coming. It would be very easy for me to say, "Well, God has not completely healed me, so I guess He is not answering my prayers," or "God has not made my songs big hits yet, so I guess He is not hearing my prayer." God IS healing me one step at a time. God is still sending me songs. His purpose is known unto Him so who am I to question it. I will not allow my circumstances to outweigh His mercy!

The third person is the one who accepts the voice of God and what it has to say, and the Word takes root and blooms in them only to eventually be choked out by the world and the mockers. Have you ever had someone who says to you, "God did not do that; the doctors did." Or maybe it was more like "God would not tell you something like that. You must be dreaming." We hear those words, and we stay quiet after that about what God has done or what He has said. Why? Because the world chokes God's word right out of us. The voice of the Lord becomes silenced in that particular case because we were intimidated by the voices of this world.

And the last, of course, are those that hear the Word and take it in. They study it and know that it was God who was talking to them. They stick with it and grow and are fruitful because of it. We need to be the ones that take in the word and act upon it. Don't let the world or your problems or anything else rob you of what God has said. Only you know what God has said to you. It is important to seek Godly counsel in the form of a pastor or mentor on critical decisions as long as you know those people you are asking are filled with the wisdom of God. But remember – if you are going to do that, be ready for God to speak through those people!

Always keep in mind that His still, small voice is the one that created the universe. It is the voice that hung the stars in place. It is the voice that started the earth, sun and, stars rotating in their own ways. His voice is the most powerful force in the universe, and He is speaking to you on a regular basis.

Psalm 46:10 says,
   "Be still and know that I am God."

> *"His voice is the most powerful force in the universe, and He is speaking to you on a regular basis."*

It is in the stillness of life that He comes to us and speaks to us. Make sure that in your prayer time, you allow time for God to speak to you!

The last thing I want to mention is out of Exodus 29:20 where we read that the ears of the priests were anointed. Are your ears anointed to hear the word of God? Faith has to be applied to hearing just as much as it does to anything else because without faith, it is impossible to please God. Are your ears ready to hear with faith, nothing wavering, or is your faith double-minded? Will you accept the voice of the Lord when it comes, or will you toss His words up in the air and say I'm not sure whether that's God or not? Are you ready to accept

His response even if it goes completely against what you would like?

We Must Accept the Response

So far, we have learned how to ask by using the A.S.K. Principle, how we can be heard and understood, that we should expect a response, and how we must listen for a response. The last step in communication is accepting the response. Notice I am not saying agree with the response. Just accept the response as the words the responder (in this case God) is sending back to us. There is a big difference, and this is very important.

We may not agree with the response someone gives us. I get into conversations with my wife sometimes where she is trying to point out that pride has risen up in me once more, and I am defending my position because of it. I gave her permission years ago to let me know when I am walking in pride, and I also have been very good at accepting her response and recognizing the pride once she has told me about it. Most of the time, I agree with her response as well, but this time I didn't. I did not think I was stuck in pride, and I told her as much. Calmly and reasonably, I told her why, and she accepted that. But this time neither of us agreed with the response of the other. We let it go at that.

The same can be true of responses we get from God. He may tell us to wait. It is rare we will agree with that response, but we still have to accept it or we will find ourselves arguing with God! It's very rare we will win that argument. Moses won a couple arguments with God, but I can't think of anyone else who did. I'm much better off to accept the response than to try and argue to get a different one.

Our communication with God can be on a multitude of subjects, and it would take forever to cover them all here. We pray about all kinds of things each day, and God will answer those on an individual basis with specific detail. God can answer many requests with yes or no or wait. These are the three most common answers. We usually don't like the wait and abhor the no, but each time it is imperative to stand back and look over the situation, remembering that God does all things for our good (Rom 8:28). If He says no, there is a good reason behind it. If He says wait, perhaps He is allowing our faith to be built as we develop patience (James 1:2-4). Patience does amazing things for us, and needs to grow in all of our lives.

Quite often, our answers are already in the Word, and He will respond through His Word. So today, as part of this lesson, I am going to give you some scripture that may just answer the prayer you have on your heart. Some I may comment on; others I will leave for you to enjoy. This is just a small sampling of the promises God has made to you and me. There are so many more!

If you desire success or prosperity:

Joshua 1:8.
"This book of the law shall not depart out of thy mouth; but thou shalt meditate therein day and night, that thou mayest observe to do according to all that is written therein: for then thou shalt make thy way prosperous, and then thou shalt have good success."

This verse shows us a way to success or prosperity. Both put a directive with that prosperity, though. Our souls must prosper, which requires meditating on His Word regularly, and not departing from His ways. Are there people who prosper without doing this? Absolutely, but they are not you. We must not look at what others are doing and what others have been granted by God and think we are entitled to it as well. We are all different, and God brings different things into our lives. Don't look at what someone else has and be seduced by it. Remember when Peter and Jesus were talking, and Jesus asked Peter if he loved Him three times? After that, Jesus told Peter to feed Jesus's sheep, and Peter asked, "What about John?". Jesus answered, "What is that to you?" (John 21:15-22). Not everything is for everyone.

Psalm 1:1-3.

Blessed is the man that walketh not in the counsel of the ungodly, nor standeth in the way of sinners, nor sitteth in the seat of the scornful.

2 But his delight is in the law of the LORD; and in his law doth he meditate day and night.

3 And he shall be like a tree planted by the rivers of water, that bringeth forth his fruit in his season; his leaf also shall not wither; and whatsoever he doeth shall prosper.

Psalm 1:1-3 has three things that will make us like that tree that is doing so well: Don't take ungodly council. Don't hang out with sinners all the time, and don't be someone who is always complaining. Then he comes back to the importance of meditating in the Word. The Word has our answers if you will just take the time to read them!

If you need healing and good health:

3 John 2.

"Beloved, I wish above all things that thou mayest prosper and be in health, even as thy soul prospereth"

Exodus 15:26.

"And (God) said, If thou wilt diligently hearken to the voice of the LORD thy God, and wilt do that which is right in his sight, and wilt give ear to his commandments, and keep all his statutes, I will put none of these diseases upon thee, which I have brought upon the Egyptians: for I am the LORD that healeth thee."

Prov 4:20-22.

"My son, attend to my words; incline thine ear unto my sayings.

21 Let them not depart from thine eyes; keep them in the midst of thine heart.

22 For they are life unto those that find them, and health to all their flesh."

Once again, we see a promise tied to being in the Word and meditating on the things of God. Perhaps this is why there are so many sick among us? We have neglected His Word and have forgotten these promises come with requirements. They are not freely given. I know Jesus died, and the stripes on His back are all I need for my healing. That is what I hear all the time. I agree to a point, but if that is true, why would God say to be in His Word, or that our soul needs to prosper for good health to be applied? Perhaps if we would be in the Word more, we would not have so many occasions to need His healing! Have you ever thought of it that way?

If you need wisdom to make a decision:

Prov 3:5-6.
> *"Trust in the L<small>ORD</small> with all thine heart; and lean not unto thine own understanding.*
>
> *[6] In all thy ways acknowledge him, and he shall direct thy paths."*

Prov 9:10.
> *"The fear of the L<small>ORD</small> is the beginning of wisdom: and the knowledge of the holy is understanding."*

James 1:5-7.
> *"If any of you lack wisdom, let him ask of God, that giveth to all men liberally, and upbraideth not; and it shall be given him.*
>
> *[6] But let him ask in faith, nothing wavering. For he that wavereth is like a wave of the sea driven with the wind and tossed.*
>
> *[7] For let not that man think that he shall receive any thing of the Lord."*

Anyone who has known me for a while knows that Proverbs 3:5-6 is my life verse. I stand by it, meditate on it, and apply it to everything in my life. I believe that is why I can honestly say I do not have bad days. I do not have days that seem unfulfilling. I do not have days that I do not feel God near to me. It is because I acknowledge His hand in everything in my life – the hills and the valleys, the good times and the bad. I acknowledge Him, and I know every situation is for my good.

There is never a time I do not believe that. As a result, His hand guides me, and He gives me wisdom in every circumstance. I fear Him in the sense that I am in awe of Him all the time. I am in awe of His mercy and His grace and His love.

When you ask for wisdom, do not doubt for a minute that He will give it to you. He will guide you to the truth about any situation. His wisdom comes in softly and it is found in His Word. Read and meditate on Psalm 119. You will see just how much His Word is important to you!

If you need peace:

Phil 4:6-7.
> *"Be careful for nothing; but in every thing by prayer and supplication with thanksgiving let your requests be made known unto God.*
>
> *⁷ And the peace of God, which passeth all understanding, shall keep your hearts and minds through Christ Jesus."*

John 14:27.
> *"Peace I leave with you, my peace I give unto you: not as the world giveth, give I unto you. Let not your heart be troubled, neither let it be afraid."*

Psalm 29:11.
> *"The LORD will give strength unto his people; the LORD will bless his people with peace."*

Why do we run around with no peace in our hearts or lives when Jesus says He left His peace here for all of us to enjoy?

The Lord blesses His people with peace! Why are our lives in such turmoil all the time? Don't we know that His peace is right here, resting in His hands for us to enjoy when we need it? The problem is that we have our minds on our problems, and not on Jesus, who is our peace. We have to set our minds and thoughts in a different place. We have to set our minds where Paul tells us to in Philippians.

Philippians 4:8.
"Finally, brethren, whatsoever things are true, whatsoever things are honest, whatsoever things are just, whatsoever things are pure, whatsoever things are lovely, whatsoever things are of good report; if there be any virtue, and if there be any praise, think on these things."

Think on these things, not your troubles, cares, or worries. Think on these things! Philippians 4:4-8 is a powerful portion of scripture that I urge you to meditate on for a long time if you are not familiar with it. Knowing these verses and putting them into practice will change your whole outlook on life. If you live a life filled with turmoil, worry, doubt, fear, complaining and arguing, do this today! After meditating on these verses for a week or so, you will see a change come your way. I guarantee it because It's God's Word.

If you need more patience:

James 1:2-5.
"My brethren, count it all joy when ye fall into divers temptations;

³ Knowing this, that the trying of your faith worketh patience.

129

⁴ But let patience have her perfect work, that ye may be perfect and entire, wanting nothing."

I have heard it said, and you probably have to, that we should never pray for patience because trials will come. I will say this: Trials will come no matter what you pray for, and then you will be wishing you had more patience. We talked extensively about patience and waiting when we discussed Knocking. When I studied out these verses in James and asked the Lord for wisdom, I came to this conclusion.

We count it joy when troubles come because through those trials, our faith is tried and tested. That trying and testing of our faith makes our faith stronger, and in the process we learn to be patient waiting for God to bring a solution to the trials, which we know He will. Patience will bring us to the point that we are perfected and are ready to do the task God has for us next.

Trials will not only bring us patience but should bring us joy as well. The growth that comes into our life through trials could not be replaced with anything else. They are truly a blessing! We know that when we have that patience, Isaiah 40:31 becomes a reality:

"But they that wait upon the LORD shall renew their strength; they shall mount up with wings as eagles; they shall run, and not be weary; and they shall walk, and not faint."

I hope you are getting the idea. I could go on for hundreds more pages, because there are that many promises God has given us in His Word. What I wanted to show you is that many times, your answer is right there if you just get into the Word. We wait and wait, thinking God is not going to answer or that He doesn't hear us, when all the while He has provided the answer a long time ago. We just haven't taken the time to find it.

Spend time with God daily. Get into the Word. When you have a need, look up scriptures that provide you insight into your answer. Then believe without any doubt that this Word is for you. Accept the answer God has given. Apply Proverbs 3:5-6 to your daily life. You will find that the answer is always right there, waiting for you, and that your prayers are always answered – Always.

Chapter 4

When Should We Pray

I know what you are going to say. We should pray anytime the Holy Spirit moves us to pray, and you would be right. We will be talking about that. But there are several scriptures that show us the importance of having a regular prayer time and not just relying on the Spirit to prompt us. I am going to admit here that this is one of my weak points as a follower of Christ, and I am praying and hoping this teaching will spur me on to a better, regular practice of prayer.

I would guess we all have people in our lives who we regularly pray for, like friends, family, church attendees, people who have been mentioned to you through the week, etc. These prayers should be prayed at a set aside time during the day when we bring our requests to the Lord. We have already laid out the principles of prayer, so you are armed and dangerous to the enemy. When you take these requests to the Lord is your decision, though, and an act of your will.

The morning is my preferred time. I find that if I wait until later in the day, I get caught up in my daily activities, and the time passes by me. Before I lift my head from my pillow, I pray for those in my life that I want blessed every day. This has always worked best for me.

Mark 1:35.

> *"And in the morning, rising up a great while before day, he went out, and departed into a solitary place, and there prayed."*

Here, we see that Jesus used this time for prayer. He arose before anyone else and got by Himself. One of the main reasons I believe He did this is that during the day, He was always crowded around with people – either the twelve disciples or the throngs of people who came for healing and teaching. If He tried to wait until later to pray, it would be very difficult to get away, although He was able to on occasion. I believe this was a regular routine with Jesus, not just a one-time thing. Our prayer time should be a regular routine with us as well.

Psalm 5:3.

> *"My voice shalt thou hear in the morning, O Lord; in the morning will I direct my prayer unto thee, and will look up."*

Psalm 119:147.

> *"I prevented the dawning of the morning, and cried: I hoped in thy word."*

These words of David also tell us that the morning is a good time to bring our requests before God. There are many scriptures that discuss praising the Lord in the morning as well. I believe this is the best time for both of these practices. Our mind is clear and we are ready to face another day. Not only do we need to pray for those other people, but we need guidance to go through the day. Where would I be without God's guidance during the day? I really don't want to find out!

If we wait until later in the morning or afternoon, the cares of this world have come in and filled our mind with everything but those requests we need to take to the Lord. At least this is what happens to me. If I don't take this time in the morning, it rarely gets done! Don't let the day steal away your time and push these things out of your schedule.

Mark 6:46-47.

"And when he had sent them away, he departed into a mountain to pray. ⁴⁷ And when even was come, the ship was in the midst of the sea, and he alone on the land."

We see here Jesus asking the people to depart. He had just fed 5,000 people miraculously with 5 loaves and two fishes. I am sure the people were reluctant to leave, but they did. He then told the disciples to get into the ship and go to the other side as He stayed behind to pray. It was probably late afternoon or early evening when He started to pray, and He prayed into the night.

My best friend sets aside time around 3:00 every day to pray. He is as regular as anyone I know at keeping this time. I applaud him for being able to block out this time to go to the Lord. I also know his prayers are heard and answered because he has prayed for me incessantly through this cancer battle and has brought many victories to my life. Thank you, Jason!

I would guess Jesus did not get this opportunity too often and enjoyed it when He did. Afternoon prayer times are difficult because of the demands of life that kidnap our schedules. We, like Jesus, would have to send everything else away in order to get alone with God. That is not easily done.

1 Samuel 15:11.

"I regret that I have made Saul king, for he has turned back from following Me and has not carried out My commands "And Samuel was distressed and cried out to the LORD all night."

This verse tells us right up front why Samuel went to God all night. Saul had messed up once again, and now Samuel would have to find a replacement and go against the King. Not an easy thing, even for a prophet! So He spent the night in prayer and shortly after this He anointed David King in Saul's place. There are times a situation lays heavy on our heart and we are kept awake at night or The Holy Spirit wakes us in the middle of the night to pray. These times of prayer are precious and anointed. Take full advantage of them.

Luke 6:12.

"And it came to pass in those days, that he went out into a mountain to pray, and continued all night in prayer to God."

After He healed a man in the synagogue, Jesus departed and prayed all night. Have you ever been to an all-night prayer meeting? I haven't in years, but I remember them as being powerful when I did go. However, this was a prayer meeting of one. Jesus prayed all night! I would most likely fall asleep. It takes tremendous dedication to stay up all night praying. I would say that I could probably find enough to pray for, but each prayer would have to be extensive and with purpose.

I'm not sure exactly what He prayed about all night, but if we read on we see the next day He called the disciples to His side and then ministered healing to the masses before preaching to them. He had a full day coming up, and I think

He knew it. He stayed up all night praying and then all-day ministering! God must have given Him supernatural strength to accomplish this. I would not suggest this unless you have a directive from God to do so. He will tell you when all night prayer is to be given.

Psalm 63:6, Psalm 119:62, Psalm 119:148 all talk about praying in the night. When I wake up in the middle of the night, I take time to pray as well. Often, I can feel the prompting of the Holy Spirit at these times. It is often a time when He also gives me poetry and songs of praise.

Then there are those scriptures that teach us to pray before trouble comes in, not when it comes in. It is so important we are "prayed-up" before trials enter our lives. We will be able to handle them so much better. I am not going to put the whole portion of scripture here, but will give you some examples of this principle.

Genesis 32:9-12 – Jacob prays that God will give him favor before going to meet Esau.

Judges 11:30-31 – Jepthah prays for victory before the battle.

Judges 16:28 – Samson prays that God will be with him before the pillars are brought down.

2 Chronicles 14:11 – Asa prays for victory before the battle.

2 Chronicles 20:6-12 – Jehosaphat prays for victory before the battle.

And of course, there is Matthew 26:39-44, Mark 14:36-42 and Luke 22:39-46, where Jesus prays for God's will to be done, needing strength for what He was about to face on the cross. This was the ultimate prayer before a trial!

> *"If we pray before the storms, we won't be so concerned when they come because we will know that God is in control."*

Many people call this being "prayed up." I like to think of it as being prepared for whatever comes. So many times, we start praying when a bad situation hits us. Perhaps if we were in prayer on a more consistent level, we would not be so worried once trouble comes. Prayer has the ability not only to change the atmosphere around us, but also our internal atmosphere. If we pray before the storms, we won't be so concerned when they come because we will know that God is in control.

Then, of course, there are these verses:

Acts 6:4.
> *"But we will give ourselves continually to prayer, and to the ministry of the word."*

Acts 12:5.
> *"Peter therefore was kept in prison: but prayer was made without ceasing of the church unto God for him."*

Romans 12:12.
> *"rejoicing in hope; patient in tribulation; continuing instant in prayer;"*

1 Thessalonians 5:17.
> *"Pray without ceasing."*

Ephesians 6:18.
"praying always with all prayer and supplication in the Spirit, and watching thereunto with all perseverance and supplication for all saints;"

Philippians 4:6.
"Be careful for nothing; but in everything by prayer and supplication with thanksgiving let your requests be made known unto God."

"Continually in prayer", "Prayer. . .without ceasing", "Continuing instant in prayer", "Pray without ceasing", "Praying always", "in everything by prayer". The message is clear. We should always be in an attitude of prayer. We have discussed at length that prayer is simply a conversation with God. It does not have to be fancy or embellished.

We can come to God anytime and His ears are open to our cry. Things will come up in our lives; others will be brought to our attention that need prayer. We might get a call, or a text, or a Facebook post from someone who needs our prayers. We should always be ready to go to the Lord in prayer. The time we set aside is for those requests that are constant. The rest of the day we need to be ready to pray.

Chapter 5

How Should We Pray

Everyone knows how to pray, right? It's just talking to God, expressing our needs and the needs of others, correct? I mean, it's not rocket science, is it?

No, it is not. The Bible has many examples of different ways to pray. Are we silent, or do we pray out loud? Do we pray in the spirit or in the flesh, or do we write out our prayers? Do we stand or sit or bow? Do we come to God in humility, or do we come boldly before the throne of God? Is there a pattern of prayer that I can use? We will be exploring all of these "How's" in this chapter.

Silent Prayer

Silent prayer is probably the most common type of prayer. Most of the time, I pray silently when I am by myself and praying for those people on my prayer list (you do have a prayer list, right?). There are times that I pray aloud by myself, but most of the time I use silence. Perhaps that is something I should change. Maybe if I prayed aloud, I would be more likely to keep the routine, as this is an area that I falter in too often.

There are also silent prayers given for those who come to mind during the day or requests that come our way. We bring them to God in meetings, in church, or in the privacy of our home. Or maybe we are in the midst of a business meeting, and we are prompted to pray! Whenever they pop up, we take action on them. Here are a few verses about silent prayer in the Word:

Genesis 24:45.
"And before I had done speaking in mine heart, behold, Rebekah came forth with her pitcher on her shoulder; and she went down unto the well, and drew [water]: and I said unto her, Let me drink, I pray thee."

Jacob prayed silently for the wife Abraham had sent Him to find, and we see His prayer answered.

1 Samuel 1:12.
"And it came to pass, as she continued praying before the LORD, that Eli marked her mouth."

When Hannah prayed silently in the temple for a son, Eli wondered why her mouth moved, but no words proceeded. The result of her prayer was the birth of the prophet Samuel.

Matthew 6:6.
"But thou, when thou prayest, enter into thy closet, and when thou hast shut thy door, pray to thy Father which is in secret; and thy Father which seeth in secret shall reward thee openly."

Jesus tells us to not be public about our prayers but to pray in the closet to God, and the Father will reward us with the answer. There are times we should not tell people we are praying for them because we may take pride in that statement if the answer comes. We may think we are the cause of that answer, but we are not. God is. We help it along, but we should do it in secret. At other times, people need to know we are praying for them. Use proper judgment to determine when you should be silent, and when you should say something.

Another aspect of silent prayer is meditation. This is coming to God in our thought life, and appears throughout the Bible. Meditation is a way to communicate with God and let Him know our thoughts are on Him, or on His Word, or on those things that are pleasing to Him. I could list hundreds of verses that talk about meditation on the things of God, but I will not. I will say it is all through Psalm 119, which is a glorious Psalm that we should all read often. A few other ones that I am fond of include:

Philippians 4:8.
"Finally, brethren, whatsoever things are true, whatsoever things are honest, whatsoever things are just, whatsoever things are pure, whatsoever things are lovely, whatsoever things are of good report; if there be any virtue, and if there be any praise, think on these things"

This verse has a lot of power behind it and can shape our lives and our witness in remarkable ways. We should all do our best to live by this verse every moment of every day because what we put into our minds is what will come out. You can see why Philippians 4:8 is so important for our silent prayer, meditation and thoughts when you see what Jesus says:

Matthew 15:16-20.

> *And Jesus said, Are ye also yet without understanding?*
> *[17] Do not ye yet understand, that whatsoever entereth*
> *in at the mouth goeth into the belly, and is cast out into*
> *the draught? [18] But those things which proceed out of*
> *the mouth come forth from the heart; and they defile*
> *the man. [19] For out of the heart proceed evil thoughts,*
> *murders, adulteries, fornications, thefts, false witness,*
> *blasphemies: [20] these are the things which defile a man.*

We tend to look at alcohol, drugs and other things as defiling things that go into us, and we would be right. However, there are things in our heart that will defile us when they come out of our mouth. How important does that make it to think on those things listed in Philippians 4:8? Very important! Our thoughts will shape our prayer lives!

2 Cor 10:5.

> *"casting down imaginations, and every high thing*
> *that exalteth itself against the knowledge of God, and*
> *bringing into captivity every thought to the obedience*
> *of Christ."*

These are things we must do through prayer and meditation. Our mind is constantly drifting from one thought to another, and when it starts into those things that are ungodly, we must cast them down and bring our mind back to God. This action of prayer is typically an inner battle that is fought silently within ourselves. How do we become victorious in this battle? Reading and meditating on Psalm 119 is a good way to start.

Praying out Loud

Praying out loud is something we typically do in church or in fellowship with someone else. It can also be used in our private prayer time and is probably seen as the most effective type of prayer. Praying aloud uses two of our senses as we not only use our ears to hear, which I believe we do with silent prayer, but we also use our mouths to speak. Our words have a lot of power. Read James 3, and you will see what importance the tongue has and how powerful it can be. When we pray aloud, we speak God's word into the air, and it never leaves the atmosphere. Never downplay how powerful your words are to someone else.

Matthew 21:21.
> *"Jesus answered and said unto them, Verily I say unto you, If ye have faith, and doubt not, ye shall not only do this which is done to the fig tree, but also if ye shall say unto this mountain, Be thou removed, and be thou cast into the sea; it shall be done."*

Have you read Genesis 1 lately? God spoke and there was light. He spoke and there was the sky and the earth. He spoke the stars in place and the sun and moon into existence. All of creation came by God speaking the word. That is how powerful God sees the spoken word. He could have waved His hands, or just thought all things into being. But He spoke.

Our words are powerful as well. Speak to those mountains in your life. Speak with all faith and all authority given to you by Jesus. He says if you believe and do not doubt, it will be done. Read this story about the power of this kind of prayer:

145

A small congregation in the foothills of the Great Smokies built a new sanctuary on a piece of land willed to them by a church member. Ten days before the new church was to open, the local building inspector informed the pastor that the parking lot was inadequate for the size of the building. Until the church doubled the size of the parking lot, they would not be able to use the new sanctuary. Unfortunately, the church with its undersized lot had used every inch of their land except for the mountain against which it had been built. In order to build more parking spaces, they would have to move the mountain out of the back yard.

Undaunted, the pastor announced the next Sunday morning that he would meet that evening with all members who had "mountain moving faith." They would hold a prayer session asking God to remove the mountain from the back yard and to somehow provide enough money to have it paved and painted before the scheduled opening dedication service the following week. At the appointed time, 24 of the congregation's 300 members assembled for prayer. They prayed for nearly three hours. At ten o'clock the pastor said the final "Amen". "We'll open next Sunday as scheduled," he assured everyone. "God has never let us down before, and I believe He will be faithful this time too."

The next morning as he was working in his study there came a loud knock at his door. When he called, "Come in", a rough looking construction foreman appeared, removing his hard hat as he entered.

"Excuse me, Reverend. I'm from Acme Construction Company over in the next county. We're building a huge shopping mall. We need some fill dirt. Would you be willing to sell us a chunk of that mountain behind the church? We'll pay you for the dirt we remove and pave all the exposed area free of charge if we can have it right away. We can't do anything else until we get the dirt in and allow it to settle properly."

The little church was dedicated the next Sunday as originally planned, and there were far more members with "mountain moving faith" on opening Sunday than there had been the previous week! (Origin unknown)

Oh, that we would all have that kind of faith! Not only for physical, real mountains, but for the looming mountains and obstacles that seem to block our path at every turn. God can move them, and with applied faith, nothing wavering, we can too. When we speak to those mountains, they will move!

Isaiah 58:9.
> *"Then shalt thou call, and the L*ORD *shall answer; thou shalt cry, and he shall say, Here I am."*

Call out to Him! Cry out to Him! He will answer! He will hear! The prophet sums up the power of spoken prayer in these simple words. Why would we want to hold back?

James 5:14-15.
> *"Is any sick among you? Let him call for the elders of the church; and let them pray over him, anointing him with oil in the name of the Lord:* [15] *and the prayer of faith shall save the sick, and the Lord shall raise him up."*

The prayer of faith is the prayer spoken by the elders as they anoint with oil. This is prayer that is spoken out loud over the person, building their faith and the faith of all around. This powerful prayer will deliver the sick and raise him up.

Isaiah 65:21.
> *"And it shall come to pass, that before they call, I will answer; and while they are yet speaking, I will hear."*

This shows us that God does know our thoughts. He says before they speak I will answer. While we speak, He will hear. He wants us to speak out our needs and let Him know we understand what we have need of. He knows. Do we really know what we need? Are we praying in the Father's will, or our own? He desires to hear us!

I Peter 3:12.
> *"For the eyes of the Lord are over the righteous, and his ears are open unto their prayers."*

His ears are open, attentive, and listening to our spoken prayers. They are music to His ears. He loves to hear us call on Him. Speak out your prayers and be heard by Almighty God! You get the picture!

Written prayers

Some people like to write out all their prayers. They put them in a journal. I have never journaled. I admire people who can sit down and write out their prayer requests. It is an amazing gift, and it can serve as a reminder of prayers that are answered because you have it all written down. I think it is a great way to go about praying.

This method actually employs four of our senses, and that is why it is the most powerful form of prayer for us. We speak it in our minds, see it with our eyes, and hear it with our ears as it is put on the paper, and we feel the pen putting the words down. If you use a pen that uses strawberry ink, you can even smell the words as they go down. Utilizing all those senses puts it deeper into our memory. Any behavioral analyst will tell you that. Any communication specialist will tell you that the more senses you get your audience to use, the better they will remember your speech.

It is hard to find reference to praying by writing in the Scripture, but the Scripture is full of written prayer. The Psalms are a good place to start, of course. They are filled with prayers. The prophets wrote out prayers. There are many prayers written in the Chronicles. Look for yourselves and see if this is a discipline you might want to embark on. I often have prayers in the poems God gives me, so it is an area I use on occasion.

Praying in the Spirit or in the Flesh

1 Corinthians 14:14-15.
> *"For if I pray in an unknown tongue, my spirit prayeth but my understanding is unfruitful. [15] What is it then? I will pray with the spirit, and I will pray with the understanding also: I will sing with the spirit, and I will sing with the understanding also"*

NOTE: I understand that many who read this book may not believe in the gift of tongues as I do, but I am going to cover this from my perspective, and hopefully you will see why we of Pentecostal circles put so much stock in this gift of the Spirit (1 Corinthians 12:8-11). I pray you'll bear with me with an open mind.

Paul states that he will use both of these methods to pray – with the understanding and with the spirit. Praying with the understanding means I am praying with my own words about a situation that I am knowledgeable about. Praying with the spirit means that I am praying about something that I don't have the details about. Let me explain further.

John comes up to me and asks me to pray with him about a medical test he is going to have done tomorrow. He tells me he is a little worried because if the test comes back a certain way, he may need further tests to determine what's next. He does not want to give me any further details at this time.

In this case, I can pray with my understanding because there is a specific purpose for the prayer. I know he is going for a test and that he wants the right result, so he will not have to face future tests. I pray words that go along with that request. I take his hand and lead him in prayer, and he is grateful for my prayers.

The next day, as he is going in for the test, I will pray at my home for him, but this time, I will add a different element. I will pray with my understanding on those things I know about. I will also allow the Spirit to lead me in prayer about the specifics since I do not know the specifics of the test or what they are looking for.

Romans 8:26-27:

> *"Likewise the Spirit also helpeth our infirmities: for we know not what we should pray for as we ought: but the Spirit itself maketh intercession for us with groanings which cannot be uttered. [27] And he that searcheth the hearts knoweth what is the mind of the Spirit, because he maketh intercession for the saints according to the will of God."*

There are times I am not sure exactly what I should pray for. Now, don't get me wrong. The Spirit leads when I pray with my understanding also, but that prayer can only go as far as my knowledge will take it. The Spirit knows every detail of what John is going through, what they are looking for, what the symptoms are, and how to bring about a good solution. When I allow the Spirit to speak through me with "groanings that cannot be uttered," I am praying God's perfect will for that person because it is the Spirit that is speaking. The groanings, in our belief, are called tongues. These tongues are our prayer language. They come out when we open our mouth, and we loose our tongue to speak a heavenly language in prayer.

The big difference between the two is that praying with our understanding is reactionary. We react to the situation we have been made aware of and pray accordingly. Praying with tongues is pro-active. We are looking ahead and taking action on something we have not been made aware of. Utilizing both of these methods gives John all I have in prayer, and that will bring about an answer every time.

Ephesians 6:18 says this:
"Praying always with all prayer and supplication in the Spirit, and watching thereunto with all perseverance and supplication for all saints;"

Paul says we should always be bringing prayer before God. We discussed this in Chapter 4 on when we should pray. Prayer is the last item listed as part of our spiritual armor. It protects us from principalities, against powers, against the rulers of the darkness of this world, and against spiritual wickedness in high places. (Ephesians 6:12). This is spiritual warfare, and our prayer language is the most powerful weapon we have in this battle. I rely on it!

We should use prayer and supplication. The prayer is public, private, in church, or for family. Supplication is seeking in earnest prayer, beseeching God, pleading with Him. These need to be brought before God with persistence, not just one time. We have an obligation to pray with all we have once we have been asked. It is what holds our brothers and sisters up in their time of need. Let us pray with both the Spirit and with our understanding to get the best results.

Pray Humbly or Boldly

Both of these are very acceptable and necessary. We should always come to God with humility, recognizing Him as far superior than us. Yet there are times that we need to come boldly before the throne of God. Knowing when which approach should be used is the key.

First, let's look at the humility side. Micah 6:8 is one of the verses in the Bible that none of us should ever ignore:

> *"He hath shewed thee, O man, what is good; and what doth the* LORD *require of thee, but to do justly, and to love mercy, and to walk humbly with thy God?*

The word "requires" here means that God asks for it or demands it. It is a word that makes this as close to a commandment as could be. Seek justice, love mercy and walk humbly before your God. There is no room for pride before God, no room for unmerciful acts, no room for injustice. To effectively come to God, we need to do all we can to comply with this wonderful verse. It should be a driving force behind our lives.

I have tried walking proudly with God, and He allowed me to do so. But in the end He had to bring me down to my knees, and I realized that being prideful was not the way to please

Him. To please God, humility needs to reign in my life, and especially in my prayer life. I am in no position to demand anything from God! He has provided so much for me already that I cannot begin to make a list. He is so merciful, and yet He still tells me, "I will have mercy on whom I will have mercy (Exodus 33:19)." He has no obligation to grant my requests, and yet He does so often. We must walk in that same mercy. He desires for us to show that mercy to everyone around us.

You might say to me, "It says in His Word that if we ask, He will do it, and God always keeps His promises!" I would ask you this. Are you walking fully in every commandment and instruction in righteousness? Are you perfect as He asks you to be (Matt 5:48)? Are you holy

> *"I am in no position to demand anything from God! He has provided so much for me already that I cannot begin to make a list."*

as He is holy? (1 Peter 1:16). If not, and I doubt any of us are, He could strike us dead now if He wanted to and be fully justified! But He is merciful. If He decides to tell me to wait on that prayer request, I, in all humility, should accept that response without question or hesitation.

Matt 6:3 tells us this:
> *"But when thou doest alms, let not thy left hand know what thy right hand doeth."*

We should never boast about our giving. We should just do it and forget about it. Then Jesus goes on to say we should pray in the closet, not where everyone can see us. This takes us out of the place where we boast about the prayers we have had answered. That just stirs up pride. When we pray in secret, the Father will reward us for our obedience, and reward us openly. I believe that means He will grant our requests.

153

Romans 12:3.

"For I say, through the grace given unto me, to every man that is among you, not to think of himself more highly than he ought to think; but to think soberly, according as God hath dealt to every man the measure of faith."

Humility – always! We all have the measure of faith. Some of us just place it in different places. We discussed this earlier in our study. Our faith is built up by reading the Word and by going through trials ourselves. Humility makes us realize we need more faith to be more effective, so we continue to seek growth in the kingdom. Strive for humility in your prayer life. This is the preferred attitude of prayer. We are closer to God when we are humble before Him. Practice humility with all you have.

But then there is boldness needed at times. Hebrews 4:16 tells us this:

"Let us therefore come boldly unto the throne of grace, that we may obtain mercy, and find grace to help in time of need."

This verse is often used to justify demanding things of God. Notice the wording here very carefully. We can come boldly, but it is a throne of grace, not a treasure house of riches for us. It is grace that was provide on the cross and grace that was given freely to us already. What are we looking for? Mercy! What does God say about Mercy? He will have mercy on whom he will have mercy. It is His choice, not ours.

The last part of this verse really brings it home. Yes, we can come boldly to God with our request, but the request should not be for anything but grace in a time of need. It is not to make us rich or build up our business. We come boldly, with all humility, looking for mercy and hoping for grace to be bestowed on us in our current situation. It is not about demanding anything.

Ephesians 3:12 says this:
> *"In whom we have boldness and access with confidence by the faith of him."*

We are only allowed this boldness and this access by our faith in Christ. Because of Him, we can approach God with confidence because He has secured our access to the throne. When should we use this boldness we have been granted? Here are a few instances where boldness can be the attitude of prayer:

John 14:13-14.
> *"And whatsoever ye shall ask in my name, that will I do, that the Father may be glorified in the Son. [14] If ye shall ask any thing in my name, I will do it."*

In effect, Jesus grants us power of attorney here. If we ask in His name, He will do it. That is why we can be bold. Because He has granted us that permission. He is our mediator (1 Timothy 2:5).

2 Peter 3:9.
> *"The Lord is not slack concerning his promise, as some men count slackness; but is longsuffering to us-ward, not willing that any should perish, but that all should come to repentance."*

When we pray for the lost, we can pray with boldness because we know that God is not willing that any should perish.

Matt 9:38.
> *"Pray ye therefore the Lord of the harvest, that he will send forth labourers into his harvest."*

When we pray for God to send laborers for the harvest, we can pray boldly because God has prepared the harvest for us and wants the harvest to come in. Take special note that we do not pray for the laborers. We pray that God will send the laborers to do the work.

Joel 2:28, Acts 2:17
> *"And it shall come to pass in the last days, saith God, I will pour out of my Spirit upon all flesh: and your sons and your daughters shall prophesy, and your young men shall see visions, and your old men shall dream dreams:"*

God has promised an outpouring of His Spirit, that we will have dreamers and visionaries. We can pray boldly for the Holy Spirit to fill us with His power. We can also pray boldly for these days to come and that a great revival will sweep the land.

Romans 12:2.
> *"And be not conformed to this world: but be ye transformed by the renewing of your mind, that ye may prove what is that good, and acceptable, and perfect, will of God."*

We can pray boldly that God will transform our minds, but we must truly desire it with all our heart. In addition we must enable the process by being in the word on a regular basis. He desires for us to prove what the good, acceptable, and perfect will of God is.

In all this boldness, we must remember that our boldness must be flanked with humility. God honors humility in us, so when we come before Him with the access and confidence Christ has given us, and approach Him with our bold requests, we also understand that His mercy and grace are what grants those requests. If we forget that humility, we can easily start to think it is our prayers and our demands that are accomplishing these prayers being answered. That is very dangerous ground, my friend!

Our Posture in Prayer

Throughout the Bible, we see various forms of posture used in prayer. This chapter will look at some examples of four positions we can take before God with our prayers. All are acceptable, and I am hoping you will be able to see how each is used for specific types of prayer. This chapter enriched my prayer life because I can now understand the value of bowing, kneeling, falling on my face, or standing before the Lord with my requests. At times, I use all of these methods to communicate with God. Let's get started!

I want to take a moment here to explain that I believe worship and praise are also a forms of prayer, because they are communicating with God just as making requests are. Worship and praise are the ways we thank God and show Him our devotion. After all, in these moments we are talking to God, lifting up our voices to let Him know our thoughts and feelings. That is His favorite type of communication from us! He loves to hear our requests as well, but more than anything, He loves to hear us praise Him. These various positions in prayer also include an attitude and posture of worship and praise.

Perhaps you never looked at praise and worship that way. I know I didn't for a long time. I hope you will now see it as a sensitive and joyous time of prayer, very different from what we normally think prayer is. Having this mindset can really invigorate our prayer life – our communication with God.

Bowing

Bowing before God puts us in an attitude of reverence before the Lord. We should always approach Him with awe and wonder. Sometimes I feel we have brought God down too low, not understanding or acknowledging just how mighty and powerful He is. We have put Him in a box so we can better understand Him. He has become just a word on our lips instead of the one who inhabits our hearts. We've lost the awe and fear that was so apparent in Old Testament times, especially during the time of Moses. God was so real then, leading them with fire by night and a cloud by day. Can you imagine that?

Remembering that God is the all-powerful, all-knowing, ever present creator of all things is just a start. Do you remember the wizard on the "Wizard of Oz?" He seemed so powerful, but there was a man behind the curtain who turned out to be supposedly be a great wizard. He was a fake. There is nothing fake about the power of our God! Putting God back in His rightful position in our lives should be a priority with all of us. Bowing before Him as our King and Lord is a good start.

Abraham wanted to find a suitable wife for his son Isaac, so he sent a servant back to his homeland to find that wife. The servant prayed that God would send the woman to him with specific words that she would say. When the servant came to a well, Rebekkah fulfilled the words that the servant had prayed to hear. After she did, Genesis 24:26 says, "Then the man bowed down and worshiped the Lord" He was humbled and in awe that God would hear and answer His prayer, so he bowed down in thanksgiving to God. When God answers our prayers in such a dramatic fashion we should bow before Him as well.

Exodus 4:31.
"And the people believed: and when they heard that the Lord had visited the children of Israel, and that he had looked upon their affliction, then they bowed their heads and worshipped."

Moses had been gone for 40 years, and he returned to tell the people that God had heard their cries and was going to deliver them. Can you imagine their excitement and their awe for God? Their immediate reaction was to bow before the Lord to worship Him in thanksgiving for His mercy. Wouldn't you be amazed if God delivered you after 400 years of bondage through someone you thought was dead and gone? I remember when God delivered me from smoking after 30 years of struggling with it. The next time I was in church, I made sure I went to the altar and bowed before God to worship Him for His great deliverance. How amazing is our God?

In Exodus 12:27, the people bowed and worshipped when the Passover was announced. In Exodus 34:8, Moses bowed his head and worshipped when God met him on Mt Sanai to give the Ten Commandments.

We are told in Philippians 2:10-11 that one day,
"At the name of Jesus every knee should bow, of things in heaven, and things in earth, and things under the earth; ¹¹ And that every tongue should confess that Jesus Christ is Lord, to the glory of God the Father."

I would prefer to bow now and acknowledge Him in reverence and awe. He is an amazing God! And in that day, I will bow before Him once again, rejoicing that He has saved me and had mercy on me.

Kneeling

Kneeling before the Lord is a posture of humility. We humble ourselves before Him because He has given us such undeserved mercy. His grace has washed over us like a soothing river, bringing with it His peace, His joy, His hope, and all the blessings He bestows on us. When we kneel before Him in prayer, it is an acknowledgement that He alone can supply our needs.

1 Kings 8:54.
"And it was so, that when Solomon had made an end of praying all this prayer and supplication unto the LORD, he arose from before the altar of the LORD, from kneeling on his knees with his hands spread up to heaven."

Solomon had just completed building the temple and was at the altar bringing his prayers and supplications to the Lord, for not only the temple but for the whole nation. He was kneeling at the altar, knowing only God could bring an answer to this prayer. I can just picture Solomon in my mind as he knelt before the altar with his hands raised to heaven! Can you see him? What a glorious posture to take before God. We see this again in 2 Chronicles 6:13.

Ezra 9:5.
> *'And at the evening sacrifice I arose up from my heaviness; and having rent my garment and my mantle, I fell upon my knees, and spread out my hands unto the* Lord *my God,'*

The people had committed sin by intermarrying with the people around them instead of marrying Israelite spouses. Ezra had rent his clothes and was distraught, but he came out of that and came before the Lord, kneeling and lifting his hands to God. He prayed a prayer of supplication to God for the nation and the people. A heartfelt prayer of repentance is fitting when we kneel before our creator.

Luke 22:41.
> *"And he was withdrawn from them about a stone's cast, and kneeled down, and prayed"*

Jesus kneels and prays in the Garden, a prayer of supplication to God that the cup might pass from Him. It is also a prayer of humility, that God's will must be done, not His.

We also see kneeling in prayer in Daniel 6:10 when Daniel prayed despite the Kings' edict. In Acts 7:60, Stephen kneels down and asks God to forgive those who stoned him. If you've ever watched movies about medieval times, you have seen men come before the kind of the day and kneel before them. This was an acknowledgement that the King was greater than the man kneeling. It is a sign of submission showing that we depend on the King and are in hopes that he will have mercy on us. When we humble ourselves before the Lord, He has a ready ear to hear our cry.

Falling on our Face before God

Falling down before the Lord is a sign of surrender as you probably guess. It is a position of giving your all to Him and letting Him have His way. When we fall before Him, it is a combination of kneeling and bowing, which signifies humility and reverence. This goes one step further, though. We are as low as we can go and acknowledge that He is the only one who can lift us up. It is total dependence on God.

Deuteronomy 9:18.
> *"And I fell down before the LORD, as at the first, forty days and forty nights: I did neither eat bread, nor drink water, because of all your sins which ye sinned, in doing wickedly in the sight of the LORD, to provoke him to anger."*

You certainly can see the desperation Moses felt during this time before the Lord. This is the only record in the Bible, outside of Jesus in the wilderness, where someone went this length of time without water or bread. He was giving all he had to God to ask for His mercy because of the sins of the people. Have you ever fallen down before God for a long period of time? I can remember times when I lay before the Lord for an hour or two, but 40 days?

When Korah rose up against Moses, we see that Moses fell down before the Lord twice during that ordeal (Num 16:4 &

22). This was a difficult time for Moses, and he had to depend totally on God to bring him through it.

Joshua 5:14.

*"And he said, Nay; but as captain of the host of the L*ORD *am I now come. And Joshua fell on his face to the earth, and did worship, and said unto him, What saith my L*ORD *unto his servant?"*

Joshua and all of Israel were getting ready to attack Jericho. Joshua was alone looking over Jericho, and when he looked up, he saw a man with his sword drawn. Joshua asked if the man was for him or against him. You can see the response above. What would be your reaction if an angel of the Lord appeared before you? I would fall on my face in total surrender. What else would there be to do?

In the Revelation, Jesus appears before John, and John falls flat on his face as if he was dead (Rev 1:17). The magnificence of Christ was too much for him to bear. The glory of the Lord is a powerful thing. I think we forget that. Numbers 20:6, Lev 9:24 and 1 Kings 18:39 all show us instances where a large group of people fell before the Lord because they were confronted by His glory. There are many times I have been in services where we ask God to send down His glory, and I just wonder to myself if we really understand what would happen if He did. We would not be able to stand in such an atmosphere. Don't get me wrong. I love it when the atmosphere in a service is overpowering. The Holy Spirit can move in such a place, and feeling His presence is awesome, to say the least. Feeling the full weight of His glory coming into a service would have us all on our faces before him.

Standing

There are very few instances of people actually standing and praying to God, but what we see tells us that this position has some redeeming qualities. It is a position of boldness, unlike the other three that show reverence, submission, and humility. We will look at two examples before we close this chapter.

Mark 11:25.
> *"And when ye stand praying, forgive, if ye have ought against any: that your Father also which is in heaven may forgive you your trespasses."*

Forgiveness takes boldness, mixed with humility. Have you ever had to forgive someone who doesn't know you have something against them? First, you have to summon the boldness to approach them and tell them you have been holding something against them. Then in humility you have to ask their forgiveness for your feelings. We must forgive from deep down inside in an attitude of prayer. God doesn't forgive us and remember. He removes our sin as far as the east is from the west. When we forgive, we should do the same.

Luke 18:11.
> *"The Pharisee stood and prayed thus with himself, God, I thank thee, that I am not as other men are, extortioners, unjust, adulterers, or even as this publican."*

The boldness of the Pharisee is apparent. This is an example of a position we should not take in prayer. This is a proud position, and we should never take such a position with God. Of course it is OK to pray standing up. We can take any position in prayer. Just make sure you do it with all the reverence, humility, and surrender you can muster up. You are not petitioning your boss at work or a police officer or someone with earthly authority. You are petitioning the Creator of all things, the King of Kings, and Lord of Lords. This honor should never be taken lightly.

One more note. I love to lift my hands to God in times of worship. I would guess some of you do, and some don't. The Bible mentions raising the hands in worship many times. David, Moses, Solomon, Jeremiah, Paul, and others all mention lifting hands to the Lord. To many it is a sign of surrender to God: to others it is a sign of giving oneself to Him. I often have these feelings when I lift my hands. Most of the time, I get a picture of a young child lifting up his hands to his father, looking up at his face with adoration, wanting to be picked up and held. This is what I envision when I lift my hands to God. Heavenly Father, pick me up and hold me! I love you!

Anointing With Oil

Anointing with oil, like the laying on of hands, was a special ceremony that was used when the priests were consecrated for service. It set them apart to do the job of the priesthood. In Aaron's case it signified that he was most holy among the people of Israel. This and anointing the temple and it's furnishings are the only places the holy anointing oil was to be used. Anointing oil in the Bible was a very special mixture of myrrh, cinnamon, calamus, cassia and olive oil. Only the high priest could mix up this oil as well. It had to be kept pure, and it was a symbol of the holiness of God. It was a powerful ceremony when the anointing oil was placed on Aaron and his sons. They were then set a apart for their service to the Lord. They were honored above the Levites who ministered daily in the temple.

Leviticus 8:12.
"And he poured of the anointing oil upon Aaron's head, and anointed him, to sanctify him."

Exodus 28:41.
"And thou shalt put them upon Aaron thy brother, and his sons with him; and shalt anoint them, and consecrate them, and sanctify them, that they may minister unto me in the priest's office."

There was another oil used to anoint the leper when he was pronounced clean. In Leviticus 14:14 we read about that oil being placed on the lepers' right ear, his right thumb and his right toe. I find that fascinating. I am not going to get into the significance of those placements as it does not enhance our prayer study. You should consider it in your own study. God has a divine purpose for everything!

Psalm 23:5.
"Thou preparest a table before me in the presence of mine enemies: thou anointest my head with oil; my cup runneth over."

In this familiar portion of scripture, David says that the shepherd anoints his head with oil. The one he follows (The Shepherd) separates him for service by pouring the oil over his head. It is a matter of consecrating David for God's service. The fact that David mentions this in the beloved 23 Psalm tells me that David found this act to be one of the most important to him. We all know the 23rd Psalm speaks about God's provision and protection. Anointing with oil falls into that category.

In the New Testament we see some of the same usage for anointing with oil, but added to it is the use of this oil to pray over the sick. It is first mentioned when the disciples went out to minister two by two.

Mark 6:13.
"And they cast out many devils, and anointed with oil many that were sick, and healed them."

We have to assume that they learned this practice from Jesus. It is very unlikely the disciples would anoint with oil if they had not seen their Master and Teacher do the same. This became a common practice with them, so when James wrote his book, he included these words.

James 5:14.
"Is any sick among you? let him call for the elders of the church; and let them pray over him, anointing him with oil in the name of the Lord."

James 5:14 is probably the verse that we most associate with anointing oil. It says if we are sick that we should call for the Elders of the church. They should pray over us and anoint us with oil in Jesus name. Today we use oil that is especially bottled for this purpose in some cases, and in others it may just be olive oil. Whatever the case it's the association we make with it that's important and not necessarily the ingredients. When we are anointed with oil, it is a way to say we are consecrating this body for healing and ministry. We should desire to be anointed with oil when we are sick because it is a Biblical principle. It may seem to us to be a small, silly thing, but it is not that to God. To God is an act of our consecration and dedication to Him, and He is always pleased with that.

Laying on of Hands

One of the ways we can further strengthen our prayer lives is by utilizing the practice of laying on of hands. This practice actually goes back to the Old Testament and is used in two different ways. The first is as a sign of association for the sacrifice that was being offered. The Levites put their hands on the sacrifice and blessed it for the use that it was intended for. This could be for The trespass offering, the sin offering, the burnt offering or the meat offering. In all these cases the Levites, who were the spiritual leaders, placed their hands on the sacrifice and blessed it. This can be found in Leviticus 1:4, 3:2, 4:15 and 16:21 and several other verses.

The second way that the laying on of hands was used in the Old Testament was to anoint an individual for service. This is especially true of the Priests and Levites, but also for Kings and leaders with authority.

Numbers 8:10-15.
And thou shalt bring the Levites before the LORD: and the children of Israel shall put their hands upon the Levites: [11] And Aaron shall offer the Levites before the LORD for an offering of the children of Israel, that they may execute the service of the LORD. [12] And the Levites shall lay their hands upon the heads of the bullocks: and thou shalt offer the one for a sin offering, and the other for a burnt offering, unto the LORD, to make an atonement for the Levites. [13] And thou shalt set the Levites before Aaron, and before his sons, and offer them for an offering unto the LORD. [14] Thus shalt thou separate the Levites from among the children of Israel: and the Levites shall be mine. [15] And after that shall the Levites go in to do the service of the tabernacle of the

congregation: and thou shalt cleanse them, and offer them for an offering.

These verses in Numbers include both of the ways laying on of hands was part of the ceremony in the Old Testament. First, the people laid their hands on the Levites to consecrate them for the Lord's service. Then the Levites put their hands on the sacrifice, consecrating it and identifying themselves as the priests of Israel. They were then appointed to do the work of sacrificing the animals brought by the Israelites.

Deuteronomy 34:9.

"And Joshua the son of Nun was full of the spirit of wisdom; for Moses had laid his hands upon him: and the children of Israel hearkened unto him, and did as the LORD *commanded Moses."*

This is a scripture which shows the transference of the spirit of wisdom from Moses to Joshua. Since Moses was not going into the promised land with the people he had been leading for 40 years he needed a replacement filled with the same wisdom God had given him. Joshua was chosen the next leader. He was one of only 3 men to survive those 40 years (Caleb and Moses being the other two). This laying on of hands was done in front of the whole nation to let them know God had appointed Joshua their new leader.

In the New Testament, there are different uses for the laying on of hands as well. This practice was used by Jesus and His disciples as well as Paul. If they all thought it was important, we should take heed to its usage and practice our prayer in the same way.

Mark 10:16.
> *"And he took them up in his arms, put his hands upon them, and blessed them."*

The children had come to Jesus because they loved Him and wanted to be near Him. As they came near, Jesus stretched out His hand, placed it on each one's head, and gave them a blessing. We see this same thing in the Old testament when Jacob blessed his sons. The laying on of hands is a way to show your favor on someone and bless them. If given by someone in authority it can signify separating them for service, much as the story above with Joshua. This can be a very powerful and meaningful time when entered into with the proper spiritual attitude of worship.

Luke 4:40.
> *"Now when the sun was setting, all they that had any sick with divers diseases brought them unto him; and he laid his hands on every one of them, and healed them."*

This verse tells us that everyone who was sick and diseased was brought to Jesus. When He laid His Hands on them they were healed. I can't imagine how many people were there but there must have been a lot. His touch is a powerful thing. We still crave His touch today. We seek to be touched by the Holy Spirit when we worship and when we pray. I personally have felt His touch quite often. It's hard to described to someone who has never experienced it. It feels as if He is in the room with us. Powerful times in the Lord arrive when He is present.

Mark 16:17-18.
> *"And these signs shall follow them that believe; In my name shall they cast out devils; they shall speak with*

new tongues; ^{18} They shall take up serpents; and if they drink any deadly thing, it shall not hurt them; they shall lay hands on the sick, and they shall recover."

Jesus, in some of His last words before leaving the disciples, told them that the laying on of hands to heal the sick would follow those who believe in Him. Thus we see in Acts several cases where the disciples and Paul laid their hands on people to enhance their prayer. Here are a couple of verses.

Acts 8:17.
"Then laid they their hands on them, and they received the Holy Ghost."

Here we see the gift of the Holy Ghost is given by the laying on of hands. Again this is a transference from one person to another just like it was in the Old Testament. There's a lot of power that comes with the laying on of hands.

Acts 28:8.
"And it came to pass, that the father of Publius lay sick of a fever and of a bloody flux: to whom Paul entered in, and prayed, and laid his hands on him, and healed him."

Paul laid his hands on the father of Publius and he was healed. Once again, we see this method used to bring healing.

1 Timothy 4:14.
"Neglect not the gift that is in thee, which was given thee by prophecy, with the laying on of the hands of the presbytery."

2 Timothy 1:6.

> *"Wherefore I put thee in remembrance that thou stir up the gift of God, which is in thee by the putting on of my hands."*

In both first and second Timothy it is mentioned that Timothy received his gifts from the laying on of hands. This is the transference of power we have talked about before.

When we ask people to lay their hands on us to pray there are two things that take place. First of all, it is a way for them to associate with what we are going through. In a way it puts them in our place, and they can pray effectively for us because they are right where we are. It also gives us encouragement that somebody is praying for us. The second thing is that it signifies a transference of power from them to us. It allows the Holy Spirit to work through them in our lives. It may be a prayer for healing, or finances or for a spiritual need in my life. Whatever the prayer it is strengthened by the laying on of hands.

> *"There's a lot of power that comes with the laying on of hands."*

I would urge all of us to make sure that we are making contact with those people that we're praying for. It does not have to be a contact that's out of place. Merely laying a hand on their shoulder or taking their hand in ours is enough to give them the reassurance that we care and that we're there for them. That point of contact is more powerful than we can possibly imagine. So let's not neglect this practice.

The Pattern of Prayer

Matthew 6:9-13.

> *After this manner therefore pray ye: Our Father which art in heaven, Hallowed be thy name.* [10] *Thy kingdom come, Thy will be done in earth, as it is in heaven.*
>
> [11] *Give us this day our daily bread.* [12] *And forgive us our debts, as we forgive our debtors.* [13] *And lead us not into temptation, but deliver us from evil: For thine is the kingdom, and the power, and the glory, forever. Amen.*

Familiar – very familiar. I would venture to say Most of us can recite this prayer by heart. In many of our churches, it is spoken by the congregation every Sunday. After all, Jesus did say this prayer is for us, right?

Yes, He did. It is not that He commanded us to recite this prayer exactly as it is written in this Matthew account. Luke's account of the same prayer (Luke 11:2-4) leaves out the last line of praise. When Jesus is quoted in Matthew, He says, "after this manner therefore pray." In Luke's rendition, which was most likely said at a different time than Matthew's, Jesus is talking only to the disciples. Luke uses the words, "When ye pray, say. . ."

The difference in the language is interesting to me. In Luke, Jesus says to use these specific words and we do. We pray this prayer exactly as Jesus gave it. Matthew's rendition was given during the Sermon on the Mount, where Jesus is instructing the crowd in the ways of the Kingdom of God. At this occasion He tells them to pray in this manner, which to me does not necessarily signify the exact words.

The Lord's Prayer is not only a prayer we should pray because we follow Him. It also gives us a pattern of prayer that would be good to incorporate with every prayer we utter. Praying in this manner can mean with the same words, or it can mean by this method. This indicates the pattern of prayer Jesus used is a good outline to follow.

In this section we will take a look at that pattern. I believe following this pattern can enrich your prayer life because, after all, this is the pattern Jesus gave us! Each statement Jesus makes in this prayer is a different part of why we come before God. He brings us to every point in a short concise way. Prayers don't need to be lengthy to be effective.

Our Father – Relationship is the first part of prayer. God is our heavenly Father; Jesus is our Lord and Savior (and so much more). We begin our prayer by acknowledging our relationship and calling out to the one whom we are addressing with our prayer. There is nothing more important in our walk with God than developing a close, very personal relationship with Him. Coming to Him with every need, confiding in Him when we are hurting or discouraged, knowing His Word and what He wants us to do. These are all a part of that relationship.

Which art in heaven - signifies direction. We want our prayers aimed in the proper direction, acknowledging Him as supreme in all things. He is the one who sits on the throne, high and lifted up. He inhabits heaven and yet dwells in our hearts. Revelation 8:4 says the prayers of the saints rise with a sweet-smelling incense before Him in heaven. This is the destination of our prayers and this where the answers come from.

Hallowed by the name – Praise. Praise should always be a part of our prayer. Praise for who He is, not what He's done. I love the Psalms because David always either begins or ends with praise – every time. Our prayers should be the same – enter with praise. I will enter His gates with thanksgiving and praise!

Thy Kingdom come – Anticipation of His response, His answer, His reply. It is anticipation of a future heaven, a future walking in His ways, and a future filled with hope and love. When the Kingdom comes, we will know His presence in a greater way than ever before. We thank Him for the answer before it comes because of this anticipation.

Thy Will be done - Not my will but thine be done. This should always be a standard statement in our prayers, whether for us or someone else. I hear people praying so often for healing, financial help, deliverance, and various other things, and I do not hear them say God's will be done. If even Jesus had to pray "Thy will be done," how much more should we? Granted, all those things are promises that God will provide, but do I know if He wants to provide them at this time? Or is this trial meant to build me and grow my faith, so I need to go all the way through? It is far better to pray that God will strengthen someone until He decides to deliver them from their trouble. Thy will be done!

on earth as it is in heaven – Desire. Imagine if things were on earth as they are in heaven! No more sickness, no more pain, no tears, no death, and no sorrow. We desire for all these things to pass by us, and God will bring that in His time and in His way. All things are done in heaven by His grand design. Let the same be true in you and in your prayer life.

175

As you pray, allow your words to take on heavenly meaning and purpose.

Give us this day our daily bread - Supplication. asking God for His provision and His grace. He knows what you need each day, and He is never in short supply. The biggest need we have is food for our bodies. The biggest need we have for our souls is grace. God gives us grace for each day – only enough for that day. That is why we should never worry about tomorrow! Give us THIS DAY!

Forgive us our debts as we forgive our debtors – Mercy. The whole thing applies! God forgives us as we forgive others! We need His forgiveness every time we mess up somewhere. This is often a daily occurrence with me. But the prayer is very specific. Forgive us as we forgive our debtors. This should be part of every prayer, asking God for forgiveness and mercy and forgiving others in the process. We cannot grab onto the first part of this portion and forget the second part!

Lead us not into temptation – Guidance. I need guidance every day. Guidance to do my writing, guidance to set my schedule, and guidance to get done all that needs to be done. Daily I should ask God to direct my steps and keep me away from temptation. If temptation comes, this prayer asks that we not be lead into it. Stay outside of it, not in it!

But deliver us from evil – Deliverance. If I should get caught up in something I should not be, He promises deliverance and salvation. Like anything else, we need to ask. Asking before we get there is the best, so making this a part of our prayer is so helpful. If I should wander off the path, Lord, bring me back onto it and deliver me from my wanderings before they happen!

For thine is the Kingdom – Faith. Faith has many aspects: faith that He is in control, faith that He is Master of all and can touch any situation, faith that this is His Kingdom and He knows all that goes on within it, faith that He can supply all my needs because He is the King who sits on the throne. Pray in Faith, nothing wavering. The entire Kingdom is His, and every element in it is at His command. That should give us great comfort.

And the power - Humility. He has the power, not me. I am but nothing before Him. I need to humbly bow before Him, allowing His power to fix the situation, not my measly human power. I can do nothing to defeat the spiritual enemies at work against me. I come to Him, broken, and needy because He has the power.

And the Glory - reverence and awe. Nothing of me, Lord. Let all the glory come to you, not me. When you deliver me, I will give you the glory. I will tell others my God delivered me. I will tell others my God healed me. I will tell others my God took away my problem. He gets all the glory!

Forever – Eternally – for all time' We end with praise forever. Our prayers should always end acknowledging His power, His authority, His glory and His answers to our faith. Every time we talk about our prayers being answered, we acknowledge Him forever, not just one time or two or twelve, but forever.

Relationship, direction, praise, anticipation, God's will, desire, supplication, mercy, guidance, deliverance, faith, humility and reverence for all time. This is the pattern of prayer we should learn to practice. Not a demanding prayer of do this for me, or do that for them. A prayer that lifts His name, gives Him the glory, and puts our requests before Him.

There are many ways to prayer. I pray this chapter will help each of you get into a deeper prayer life than you already have, and that you learn to incorporate all that Jesus incorporated in the prayer we all know so well.

Chapter 6

Where Should We Pray

This chapter may sound dull to you because you know as well as I do that we can pray anywhere we want to. Most likely, we do. We pray when we have something come into our minds that needs prayer. The Holy Spirit prompts us, and we don't wait until we get to church the next time or until we are kneeling by our bed at night or when we get back to our easy chair. We pray right there, no matter where we are.

John 4:19-24.

> The woman saith unto him, Sir, I perceive that thou art a prophet. *20* Our fathers worshipped in this mountain; and ye say, that in Jerusalem is the place where men ought to worship. *21* Jesus saith unto her, Woman, believe me, the hour cometh, when ye shall neither in this mountain, nor yet at Jerusalem, worship the Father. *22* Ye worship ye know not what: we know what we worship: for salvation is of the Jews. *23* But the hour cometh, and now is, when the true worshippers shall worship the Father in spirit and in truth: for the Father seeketh such to worship him. *24* God is a Spirit: and they that worship him must worship him in spirit and in truth.

Jesus and the disciples had travelled into Samaria while on their journeys. Many would go around Samaria because of the tensions between the Jews and Samaritans, but it was on the direct route between Judea and Galilee. Jesus was not one to waste any time!

It was around noon, and they were tired. So they stopped at a well, and the disciples went into town to get some lunch and bring it back. While they were gone, a woman came to the well by herself. Usually the women would all come together, so Jesus knew this woman must be an outcast for some reason because she was by herself.

Jesus asked the woman for a drink, and she was shocked. Jews just did not talk to Samaritans, especially men to Samaritan women! She asked Jesus why He was talking to her, and Jesus told her if she knew who He was she would be asking Him for water – the Living Water that only He can supply. He went on to explain Himself, which I am not going to dwell on today, and then came the portion of scripture above. The main point I want to draw out of this scripture is the fact that Jesus says there is no particular place we will worship, but as long as the Spirit is there, we are in a place of worship.

We have talked extensively on being prepared for prayer and how we should pray. As long as we follow the truth of scripture, our prayers are effective no matter where we are. Let's take a look at the various places Jesus prayed:

On the Mountain. Matthew 6:9-13 – Jesus teaches the disciples to pray.

In The Field – Matthew 8:1-2 – Jesus comes down from the mountain and prays for a leper.

On the Street – Matthew 8:6-9 – Jesus prays for the centurion's son in the street.

In a boat on the sea – Matthew 8:26 – Jesus rebukes the wind and the waves.

With a swine herd – Matthew 8:29-31 – Jesus casts the legion into a swine herd.

In someone's house – Matthew 9:1-9 – Jesus heals the paralytic man.

In a crowd – Matthew 9:20-22 – A woman is cured from an issue of blood.

By the way-side – Matthew 20:28-34 - two blind men healed.

During a meal – Matthew 26:26-27 – Jesus prays over the bread and wine.

In a garden – Matthew 26:39-44 – Jesus prays in the Garden of Gethsemane.

On the cross – Matthew 27:46 – Jesus cried out to God.

These are just a few examples of various places Jesus prayed, and only from the book of Matthew. If I listed them all, it would take too many pages. The point I am making is that no matter where we are, we should pray when we see a need. One of the astonishing things we read is that when people came to Jesus or when He met them on His travels, He always took time to pray with them, no matter who was around or where He was. The Bible tells us He healed them all! Every leper, every blind man, every person possessed, every deaf and or dumb, every cripple, everyone sick - He healed them all.

What about you? I will confess that I am often intimidated by the world around me and don't pray when I should. When I see the lame man in Walmart, I usually don't pray for them right there. When I see someone sick at the doctor's office, I usually don't pray there. If I see an accident on the side of the road, I usually don't pray for them right there. If someone comes up to me and asks me for prayer, I don't always pray for them right there. I most often wait until I am in the comfort of my car or home, then I go to the Lord in prayer.

Jesus was not intimidated by the world. He would pray no matter who was around. He had the faith and trust in the Father that He knew the healing would take place. There was no doubt, no double-mindedness. He knew blind eyes would open, deaf would hear, lame would walk, dumb would talk, demons would leave, lepers would be healed, and the dead would be raised. Even in front of those who wanted Him dead, He did not back down. He healed them all!

Is that why we don't pray? Are we worried the prayer will not be answered? If we think it won't be answered, it won't be. James tells us that a double-minded man, one who's faith wavers, will receive nothing from the Lord (James 1:6-8). I know that this is my problem and I am guilty as charged! I don't fully believe that they will be healed by my prayer. I need my faith built. My trust in God needs to be magnified a thousand times. Then I need to step out boldly and pray for people no matter where I am or who is around me.

> *"This world needs prayer warriors and those who will step out in faith and start praying for all the hurting people around us."*

This world needs prayer warriors and those who will step out in faith and start praying for all the hurting people around us. We should pray not in the quiet of our homes, but out in the streets, in the malls, and in the highways and byways of life. Prayer warriors who don't worry about who sees or who might mock us. Will you be one of these? Will I?

Chapter 7

What Should We Pray For

I know. I know. We should pray for everything! Not a day goes by that each of us doesn't have a list of things that need our attention in prayer. We have talked about every aspect of prayer and have learned that God always answers our prayers.

In this chapter, I want to help build your faith a little more by showing you many scriptures that let us know God wants to hear our prayers and answer our prayers in various areas of our lives.

HEALING – James 5:14-15.
"Is any sick among you? let him call for the elders of the church; and let them pray over him, anointing him with oil in the name of the Lord: [15] And the prayer of faith shall save the sick, and the Lord shall raise him up; and if he have committed sins, they shall be forgiven him."

We can call for the elders, or we can pray for someone ourselves. In any case, it's the prayer of faith that saves the sick and delivers them from their illness. It is faith that does not waver, faith that is determined and persistent, faith that can move mountains, faith that has been tested and tried. This is the kind of faith we need for any prayer!

FINANCES – Joshua 1:8.
"This book of the law shall not depart out of thy mouth; but thou shalt meditate therein day and night, that thou mayest observe to do according to all that is written therein: for then thou shalt make thy way prosperous, and then thou shalt have good success."

God tells us how to be prosperous and have success. Three times in Joshua chapter 1, God tells us this. We can pray for financial needs anytime we want, but if we are not doing what God says in Joshua 1:8, then He has no obligation to answer. If we are doers of this verse and do it with all our heart, God will honor His word. After all, He magnifies His word even above His name (Psalm 138:2). It's all dandy and good that you pray in faith, but make sure you are living in faith as well!

SAFETY – Psalm 91:11-12.
"For he shall give his angels charge over thee, to keep thee in all thy ways.

[12] They shall bear thee up in their hands, lest thou dash thy foot against a stone."

The key to understanding this promise are the words "in all thy ways". If you meander off to the left or the right or if you are tempted to jump off a mountain as Jesus was (Matt 4:6), that is not your normal way. If you are staying on that straight and narrow path that leads to God, He will keep you safe. He will watch over you every second and even send angels to guard you and hold you up. If you are going to pray that God will keep you safe and protect you in a certain situation, make sure you are on the right path. That is where the protection is.

DELIVERENCE – 1 Corinthians 10:13.

"There hath no temptation taken you but such as is common to man: but God is faithful, who will not suffer you to be tempted above that ye are able; but will with the temptation also make a way to escape, that ye may be able to bear it."

The prayer of deliverance from any situation is always welcomed by God. We have to remember that God will answer that prayer in His time because He may want you to go through this trail. It may be one that has been deemed a growth opportunity. Remember what James says; Trials make our faith work so we can patiently be perfected (James 1:2-4). An answer does not always come right way, but it does come. In the meantime, we can know that God has equipped us to handle whatever He allows into our lives, so rest on that with faith!

GUIDANCE – Proverbs 3:5-6.

"Trust in the LORD with all thine heart; and lean not unto thine own understanding.

⁶ In all thy ways acknowledge him, and he shall direct thy paths."

We all need guidance from time to time. It is essential, especially if we want to stay on that straight and narrow path. We pray regularly for God to guide us through situations that we are going through now or that we know are coming up later. God says He will direct our paths – with a few things we should do first: Trust Him, don't listen to your own thinking, and acknowledge He is in everything. When we do those three things, His guidance will be at our disposal!

OTHER PEOPLE – Ephesians 6:18.
"Praying always with all prayer and supplication in the Spirit, and watching thereunto with all perseverance and supplication for all saints."

Just before this verse is the description of the armor of God we must put on. That is all for our protection against the principalities and powers of our spiritual enemy. That this verse is right after that tells me that prayers for all the saints are a crowning part of that armor. Intercessory prayer is a prayer after God's own heart. After all, he interceded for us by sending His only Son to die for us. This type of prayer is something we must do to be protected from the enemy.

GOVERNMENT – 1 Timothy 2:2-3.
"For kings, and for all that are in authority; that we may lead a quiet and peaceable life in all godliness and honesty. ³ For this is good and acceptable in the sight of God our Saviour."

It is so tempting to criticize and put down the leaders of our country for the way our government is running right now. We all know the problems we have. But God tells us to pray for them. Maybe things would be different if we would all do this one simple thing and stop the other!

WISDOM – James 1:5-6.

> *"If any of you lack wisdom, let him ask of God, that giveth to all men liberally, and upbraideth not; and it shall be given him. ⁶ But let him ask in faith, nothing wavering. For he that wavereth is like a wave of the sea driven with the wind and tossed.*
>
> *⁷ For let not that man think that he shall receive any thing of the Lord."*

We can have wisdom to understand why we are going through the trials of life or wisdom for our next decision. It can be ours if we ask in the type of faith that can move mountains. God says that here. Solomon gained wisdom that way. But if we waver in our faith, we will receive nothing from the Lord. Let us build up a powerful faith!

SPIRITUAL GROWTH – Ephesians 4:14-15.

> *"That we henceforth be no more children, tossed to and fro, and carried about with every wind of doctrine, by the sleight of men, and cunning craftiness, whereby they lie in wait to deceive; ¹⁵ But speaking the truth in love, may grow up into him in all things, which is the head, even Christ."*

I would guess most of us want to grow in our walk with the Lord. We don't want to be children in Christ. We want to grow up and be mature in Him. That will enable us to avoid the traps of the enemy. We will have more understanding in His ways. We are told here that when we speak the truth in love, we will grow in Him. Speak the truth in love – always.

KNOW GOD'S WILL – Rom 12:1-2

"I beseech you therefore, brethren, by the mercies of God, that ye present your bodies a living sacrifice, holy, acceptable unto God, which is your reasonable service.

[2] And be not conformed to this world: but be ye transformed by the renewing of your mind, that ye may prove what is that good, and acceptable, and perfect, will of God."

When we give ourselves wholly to Him and allow the Word to transform our mind, we will walk in that perfect will of God. We will go through trials with confidence in Him. The world will see how we handle the bad times, and they will know by our testimony that we walk with God. We can be in His perfect will when we continue to allow His word to work within us.

These are just a few of the verses that tell us how to pray, what is required for our prayers to be answered, and the promises that will come our way if we simply walk in His commandments. As you can see, there are other things attached to each one of these that must be fulfilled before we can claim the promise of the verse. .I believe many in the church think they can pray whatever they think they have need of, and God will supply it, no matter how they are living. These powerful promises tell us different. We have an obligation to God before He has one to us.

I could list hundreds more verses to show you what to pray for and His promises to answer. This is just my favorite selection. Perhaps you have yours as well. Make a list of them and keep them handy. Then carry this list with you wherever you go so that when an opportunity to pray comes along, you have the scriptural truth that shows you this prayer will be answered. Be one that has their prayers answered! Follow God in all you do.

Chapter 8

Conclusion

I want to start by thanking you for coming on this journey with me. It has been remarkable to go back through notes I made thirty years ago and redo this study. I have learned once again about the power of our prayers and what God asks us to do in order for our prayers to be more successful. There is much more involved than just talking to God, although that is the essence of our prayers.

I am going to start doing two things as result of going through this study. The first is to keep a list of things that I am praying for. I daily pray for dozens of various things, if not close to a hundred. I am not sure if I will get them all on this list, as some things crop up mid-day, and I'm not near my journal. I will do my best. The first thing is to find the time to make the initial list.

Once the list is made, I will go back to it and check off the ones that get answered. This is the second part of what I am going to do different in my prayer life. I may even use dates when I started praying for it and when it was answered. I have one person I was praying for to get a new job, and he got it within a week. Another job-related prayer is still in the works.

Do you keep such a list? I believe it will be beneficial for my faith. I have no plans to share it with anyone, except my wife, unless God directs me to share. Answered prayer is never something we should boast about. I keep such a list of all my poetry and another list with all the songs I have written (which needs to be updated). Why not a list of prayers?

In a quick review, we talked about what I call the A.S.K. Principal. Keep asking, keep seeking, keep knocking. Asking involves being in the right spirit when we pray, understanding what God asks of us when we pray, and making sure we are asking according to scripture. We can be silent or loud, standing or bowing, on a mountain or in a boat. We can use our own language or our heavenly language. We can pray for anything the human soul and body requires as long as we have the right attitude and lifestyle to receive from the Lord, and as long as God gets the glory and not me.

Seeking involves being in His word, praying the way the Bible teaches us to pray, finding the time on a regular basis to be before God, and regularly going to Him with our requests. It means looking at all the scriptures that address the need we have so that our faith can be built up. It means not giving up until we arrive at the answer.

Knocking means waiting patiently. It means submitting to His timetable, not our own. It means not grumbling or complaining when the answer doesn't come right way. Knocking means asking for wisdom to know what we may need to do to get to the answer. It means listening intently for God to speak and show us the answer.

We've learned that prayer is a simple conversation with God. The most important part of that conversation is listening. So often we miss the answer because we are too busy praying and don't listen to what he has to say. Prayer should be a two-way conversation!

We've learned that prayer can be made anytime, anywhere, for anything. God loves to hear our requests. What prevents us from coming to Him with our needs? It is pride mostly. We feel we can handle things ourselves. So, we don't pray about this thing or that and then find ourselves praying to get out of the jam we got into because we didn't pray. Better to pray first, I say.

At the back of this book is a list of all the scriptures used and the page you might find them on. Perhaps you have a favorite scripture and want to find out how it fits into the A.S.K. principle? Or maybe you can use this as a quick reference when you need a verse to hold onto. In any case, I hope you will use these scriptures often to enhance your prayer life.

I pray your prayer life grows as much through reading this book as mine did by writing it. Pouring through all these scriptures can't help but build your faith! Let us all go from here and make a better world through our prayer!

Endnotes

1. Francois de Salignac de La Mothe-Fenelon. *The Seeking Heart.* SeedSowers Publishing

Several times throughout this study I have mentioned the poetry God has given me. If you enjoy poetry, please visit either my website at **https://psalmistpetegardner.com** or my Facebook page at **https://www.facebook.com/ PsalmistPeteGardner**.

A.S.K. Principle Scripture
Cross Reference

Scripture	Page(s)	Scripture	Page(s)
Genesis 3:9-13	30	1 Kings 18:39	163
Genesis 4:9-15	30	1 Kings 19:11-12	114
Genesis 11:1-9	80	2 Kings 19;20	59
Genesis 11:6	80	1 Chronicles 16:11	62
Genesis 17:15-19	30	1 Chronicles 28:9	68
Genesis 18:16-23	38	2 Chronicles 6:13	161
Genesis 18:23-33	30	2 Chronicles 7:14	27,35,63,87,100
Genesis 20:17	39	2 Chronicles 14:11	137
Genesis 24:26	159	2 Chronicles 19:3	64
Genesis 24:45	142	2 Chronicles 20:6-12	137
Genesis 32:9-12	137	2 Chronicles 26:5	169
Exodus 3:11-4:17	30	Ezra 9:5	161
Exodus 4:31	159	Job 38-42	30
Exodus 12:27	159	Psalm 1:1-3	125
Exodus 15:26	126	Psalm 4:1	27
Exodus 20:18-21	117	Psalm 5:3	134
Exodus 28:41	166	Psalm 22:3	63
Exodus 29:20	122	Psalm 23:5	166
Exodus 32:14	39	Psalm 19:14	40
Exodus 32:30-35	30	Psalm 29:3-9	116
Exodus 33:19	153	Psalm 29:11	128
Exodus 34:8	159	Psalm 34:10	68
Leviticus 1:4	168	Psalm 34:15	98

Ezekiel 18:31	96	Mark 11:23-24	104
Daniel 2:17-18	59	Mark 11:24	91
Daniel 6:10	161	Mark 11:25	164
Daniel 6:16-20	39	Mark 14:36-42	137
Daniel 10:11-14	76	Mark 16:17-18	89,170
Hosea 10:12	64,95	Luke 1:21	112
Joel 2:12-13	97	Luke 3:15	112
Joel 2:28	156	Luke 4:40	170
Amos 5:4	70	Luke 6:12	136
Micah 6:8	152	Luke 10:19	89
Zephaniah 2:3	66	Luke 11:2-4	173
Matthew 4:1-11	118	Luke 14:10	90
Matthew 4:6	186	Luke 15:11-32	68
Matthew 5:5	65	Luke 18:1-8	60,72
Matthew 5:48	153	Luke 18:11	164
Matthew 6:3	153	Luke 22:39-46	137
Matthew 6:6	142	Luke 22:41	161
Matthew 6:7	92	John 1:1-14	82
Matthew 6:8	49	John 4:19-24	179
Matthew 6:9-13	173,180	John 5:2-4	109
Matthew 6:32	35	John 10:1-5	118
Matthew 6:33	66,70	John 14:12-14	51,80,155
Matthew 6:34	70	John 14:26	119
Matthew 7:7-8	42	John 14:27	128
Matthew 7:7-11	49,80	John 15:7	50
Matthew 8:1-2	180	John 15:16	55
Matthew 8:-6-9	181	John 16:23-27	56,82
Matthew 8:23-27	103	John 21:15-22	125
Matthew 8:26	181	Acts 2:17	156
Matthew 8:29-31	181	Acts 3:5	113
Matthew 9:1-9	181	Acts 6:4	28,138
Matthew 9:20-22	181	Acts 7:60	161
Matthew 9:38	156	Acts 8:17	171
Matthew 13:10-23	65,119	Acts 9:4-6	30
Matthew 15:16-20	144,87	Acts 12:5	58,138
Matthew 17:20	104	Acts 28:8	171
Matthew 18:4	90	Romans 2:28-29	88

CPSIA information can be obtained
at www.ICGtesting.com
Printed in the USA
BVHW040040241218
536056BV00007B/17/P

9 781545 651438